PRINCE CHARLIE

APPLETON BIOGRAPHIES

CHARLES EDWARD STUART

From the portrait by Antonio David in the
National Portrait Gallery

PRINCE CHARLIE

De Jure CHARLES III, KING OF SCOTLAND, ENGLAND, FRANCE, AND IRELAND

By

COMPTON MACKENZIE 1882-

NEW YORK

D. APPLETON AND COMPANY

1933

C. 4 75 M.

X
13₇7

To the
REVEREND JOHN MACMILLAN OF BARRA

IN WHOSE HEART THE PRINCE LIVES

Do'n
URRAMACH MAIGHSTIR
IAIN MAC ILLE MHAOIL BHARRAIDH

AIG AM BHEIL AM PRIONNSA BEO 'NA CHRIDHE

AUTHOR'S NOTE

IT was tempting for one late in the field as a biographer of Charles Edward Stuart to essay an indirect method of approach to his subject, in accord with to-day's fashion. Yet when it came to the point of adopting such a method it seemed out of place in writing of a man who was the embodiment of direct action, and it was abandoned in favour of a plain tale.

It has been the privilege of those small nations we class together as Celtic to martyr themselves in turn for an ideal, the outward visible form of which varies, but the inward spiritual meaning of which is constant. These martyrdoms have stored up a treasure of spiritual force which has nourished and sustained our European civilization. Such a martyrdom was the Rising of 1745, and from the later life of Prince Charlie we may learn the insignificance in eternity of material failure.

A word of gratitude is due to Mr. J. L. Campbell, Yr. of Inverneil, who most kindly allowed me to see the proofs of his forthcoming book, 'Highland Songs of the Forty-Five,' translated from various Gaelic poets. Ignorance of that literature has led historians and romancers into a complete misapprehension of the motives which inspired the Clans to follow their Prince, and thus into an equally complete misunderstanding of the bitterness in the heart of Charles himself when the adherence of men like Lord George Murray and the consequent mixture of motives ruined the Cause.

ARDUEENISH,
  ISLAND OF BARRA,

CONTENTS

PROLOGUE

NONE in that tragic line of Royal Stuarts, not even the Queen of Scots herself, has given to the stage of history so tragic a figure as Charles Edward Louis Philippe Casimir Stuart, who is known to the majority as Prince Charlie because that was how in English sounded the Gaelic Teàrlach, his name to those whom he loved best and by whom he was best loved.

A childhood full of bright promise, a youth of energy and daring, a prime that but for fortune's malice might have shown to the world another Alexander, a maturity of restless masquerade, an embittered middle-age fading slowly into a disillusioned senescence, such in brief is the tale of his life.

TO THE STUDENTS:

The fact that this volume is being used by the Christian Heritage College does not mean that the school necessarily endorses its contents from the standpoint of morals, philosophy, theology, or scientific hypotheses. The position of Christian Heritage College on these subjects is well known.

In order to standardize class work, it is sometimes necessary to use textbooks whose contents the school cannot wholly endorse. You understand, of course, that acceptable textbooks in certain academic fields are very difficult to secure.

CHRISTIAN HERITAGE COLLEGE
San Diego, California

I

THE MARRIAGE OF JAMES AND CLEMENTINA

The spirit of romance left nothing undone to prepare the way for the advent of the most romantic personality in the eighteenth century. The very incidents that accompanied the marriage of James VIII. and III., King of Scotland, England, France and Ireland, to the Princess Maria Clementina Sobieska seem to have strayed into history from some chronicle of knight-errantry.

After the dismal failure of the Rising of 1715, due primarily to the wretched leadership of the Earl of Mar, it was felt as a matter of imperious necessity that the exiled King should marry. The claims of various princesses were discussed, and the choice finally fell on one of the three grand-daughters of the paladin, John Sobieski, who with his mighty charge of Polish chivalry drove the circumcised hordes back from the

3

gates of Vienna and saved Europe from the Turk.

To woo a bride for his King was sent Charles Wogan, an Irish gentleman of ancient lineage, who at nineteen had been taken prisoner at Preston, had been condemned to death, and had escaped from Newgate. Wogan discovered the Sobieski princesses in Silesia. He found that the youngest and the most attractive of them had been dreaming all her girlhood of becoming Queen of England one day, and he at once chose her in preference to her sisters Casimire and Charlotte. Clementina was as happy as a princess in a fairy tale. When Wogan returned to Italy with news of the prospective bride to whose beauty and youth was added a fortune that included the famous Sobieski rubies, James wished to send the debonair Irishman back immediately to settle the affair. This intention roused one of those outbursts of petty jealousy which were almost continuous at the Court of the exiled King. Wogan was an Irish Catholic, and the Duke of Mar (he had been created a duke by James on the old-established British principle of rewarding failures) as a Protestant Scot considered him the wrong envoy to negotiate the marriage. So John Murray, the brother of Lord Mansfield, who was himself later on created Earl of Dunbar, was sent in Wogan's place to treat with Prince James Sobieski for the hand of his daughter.

Owing to this delay the secret of the proposed marriage became known to Hanoverian spies, and the *de facto* British Government threatened the Emperor, who was Clementina's cousin, that they would oppose his designs on Sicily if he allowed Clementina to travel through Austria to Italy. Meanwhile, in the autumn of 1718 James had sent off Colonel John Hay to meet his bride and escort her south, but by this time the Emperor had moved. Clementina and her mother were under arrest in a convent at Innsbruck. Hay returned to Italy alone.

On hearing the news of the arrest Charles Wogan, whom we may suspect of being in love with Clementina himself, begged the privilege of being allowed to rescue her. It was the gesture of a perfect knight, for failure would have meant his being surrendered to the English rope that was waiting for him. James accepted his offer and entrusted him with the diamonds and pearls of his mother, Mary of Modena, as a wedding present to his bride. Wogan disguised himself as a travelling merchant, got into communication with Clementina at Innsbruck, and thence made his way to Silesia to obtain the consent of Prince James Sobieski for the desperate enterprise. Clementina's father was won over by the quixotry of Wogan, who early in 1719 found three brother officers of Dillon's Irish regiment to help him 'make war upon the Emperor.' Wogan, with Major Gaydon, Captain O'Toole and Captain Misset, with whom travelled Mrs. Misset, four months gone with child, and her maid Jenny, left Strasbourg and reached Innsbruck on a snowy April night.

To cut the story short, regretfully, for the details as related by Wogan himself are of entrancing interest, Jenny was smuggled into the convent to pretend to be a princess, and the Princess herself was smuggled out in the guise of a maid. Clementina had no luggage except some pious books tied up in an apron and her portion of the crown jewels. In her excitement she fell into a gutter, lost her shoe, and had to change her clothing at the inn. When the party, with Mrs. Misset as chaperon, were some way on the road in a great hooded *berline,* Clementina remembered that she had left the jewels on the table in the inn parlour. O'Toole had to ride back for them. Luckily, he was a strong giant of a man, for he had to lift the inn gate off its hinges in order to enter without knocking. The journey across the Alps was a nightmare. The *berline* broke down, and the journey had to be resumed in a waggon. The Princess of Baden, who was travelling in front of them, was using all the available post-horses. There seemed no chance of reaching Italy before they were overtaken by the Emperor's emissaries in hot pursuit. Back in Innsbruck Jenny the maid was cleverly pretending to be a real princess, and thus she managed to gain a day and a night for the fugitives by refusing to interview the police officer whose duty it was to see that Clementina was still locked up in the convent. When at last the first courier overtook the eloping party, Misset and O'Toole intercepted him, made friends, and left him blind drunk at a wayside inn.

In the end Bologna was safely reached, and in May Clementina was wedded by proxy to

King James, who was himself busy in Spain in connection with the abortive expedition of 1719 which came to an end in Glenshiel. The King of Spain by a happy stroke of humour appointed Wogan Governor of La Mancha, and King James made this second Quixote a baronet.

II

THE BIRTH OF CHARLES

EXCEPT for Wogan's exploit and the Royal marriage, 1719 had been a bad year for Jacobite hopes. The death of Charles XII. of Sweden, a personal enemy of the Elector, and the fiasco of the Spanish landing in Loch Duich had left them languishing. On December 20th, hopes were revived by the birth of a son to James and Clementina in Rome. Mindful of the Whig lies about his own birth, James took precautions against any more warming-pan stories, and the Queen's confinement was attended by representatives of European Governments, by Cardinals and Ministers of State. A medal was struck with the motto *Spes Britanniae*. Heaven itself seemed to rejoice, for a new star appeared, and on the night the Prince was born Hanover was ravaged by a storm. The birth of an heir alarmed the Elector on his unstable throne. For the next two years there was much Jacobite

activity in England during the discontent that
followed the bursting of the South Sea Bubble
in 1720, the value of which, as an omen of what
was in store for the material civilization that
was being created by triumphant Whiggery, is
not perhaps even yet beheld in all its menacing
significance to the present state of mankind.
Arrests were numerous.   The Duke of Norfolk
was sent to the Tower.   The dauntless old
Bishop of Rochester was banished from the
country, and his chaplain, George Kelly, kept
his assailants at bay with a sword while he burnt
the compromising papers of the Atterbury Plot
in a candle's flame before he went to an imprisonment of fourteen years in the Tower.

The only victim was Christopher Layer, who
on November 30th, 1722, was condemned to
be hanged, drawn, and quartered, but was kept
alive till May 28th, 1723, in the hope of wring-
ing evidence out of him against the suspected
conspirators.   Layer was an English barrister
who had planned to abduct the Elector and de-
port him to Hanover.   He was accused of in-
triguing with Mrs. Hughes, the Prince's nurse,
to bring the baby Charles to Scotland, there to
be proclaimed.   Layer when condemned ex-

pressed a hope that he would die like a gentleman and a Christian. That prayer was granted.
His speech on the scaffold shows what kind of
men there were to devote themselves to that
baby Prince as yet unconscious of his destiny
in the gloomy Palazzo Muti where he had been
born, and where ultimately, sixty-six years
hence, he was to die:

'I come here to suffer an ignominious Death; but
not for an ignominious Crime, but for following
the Dictates of my Conscience, and endeavouring
to do my Duty. As I die for so doing, I doubt not
but I shall soon be happy; but am certain this
Nation can never be so, nor even easy, until their
lawful King is plac'd upon his Throne. I forgive
every Body, and desire Forgiveness from God for
my Sins, and from Men for what Injuries I may
have done them.'

It is noteworthy that Christopher Layer was
a Protestant.

The Anglo-Hanoverian Government's chief
spy in Rome was Philip de Stosch, a Prussian
baron who traded under the pseudonym of
John Walton. The reports written over a
period of thirty years by this rascal, whom even
Horace Walpole calls 'a man of most infamous
character in every respect,' fill several volumes.

The present writer, who has had a wide first-hand experience of this type of humanity, is not impressed by the baron's value as a witness, and that so many historians should have greedily accepted his reports illustrates the lack of worldly wisdom by which the average historian is handicapped. No history indeed has suffered more than that of Jacobitism from exploitation at the hands of academic prigs and provincial Whigs, whose unctuousness of comment is often as nauseous as castor-oil.

This is not the book in which to embark upon a discussion of the unhappy quarrel between James and Clementina. It is enough to say that there is no evidence of any kind to support the charge of infidelity against the King, and it is clear that some of the spies, who John Walton boasted were in his pay inside the Palazzo itself, helped to foment the wretched state of affairs which soon after the birth of Henry, Duke of York, in 1725, led to Clementina's leaving her husband and taking refuge in a convent. It is equally clear that Clementina herself, who as a child had set her heart on becoming Queen of England, was disappointed by the shadow of a Court in which she could merely reign emotionally. We know that she was intensely jealous, and the King's determination to have his elder son educated by both Protestant and Catholic tutors may have appeared to her an excuse to keep Colonel Hay, whom James had now created Earl of Inverness, near enough to his person to allow that fancied intrigue with Lady Inverness to be facilitated. That Clementina was intensely devout is unquestionable; but it was a selfish devotion, and it seems certain that her behaviour instead of strengthening her elder son's Catholicism did much to weaken it.

Jacobite hopes languished again during these years when everything was being done to discredit in Great Britain the Court in Rome. In 1727 the Elector could feel when he landed in Holland on his way to Hanover that his triumph was complete. At the frontier he was met by the servant of his unhappy wife Sophia, who had died in that dripping castle of Ahlden where she had been kept so many years. Into the Elector's hand he put the last message of his dying wife which summoned him to meet her before the throne of God.

'To Osnabruck!' cried George.

13

And that very midnight at Osnabruck he died from a surfeit of melons on top of a heavy supper.

At the same time as the Elector's ghost was travelling to keep that fearful tryst, Clementina, after being threatened by the ecclesiastical authorities with deprivation of the Sacraments, was returning to her husband.

It is interesting to note how Duncan Forbes of Culloden, whose obliquity of vision nearly twenty years later was to make him the arch-destroyer of his country, regards the Jacobite Court in Rome. As Lord Advocate he writes from Scotland to the Duke of Newcastle on June 26th, 1728:

'I told your Grace this last season that the dis-affection in this part of the kingdom was wearing out apace, and that the greatest part of those people who within these seven years last past were extremely violent and determined on the side of the Pretender had changed their note and *become exceedingly lukewarm and indifferent to his interests,* and now it is with great pleasure I can assure your Grace from the observations of persons that I can safely trust that the zeal with which they lately were fired is, *from a more perfect knowledge of their idol's personal character, turned into a sort of shame and confusion* for having espoused so warmly his cause; that all endeavours to support

14

his party have ceased; that the most disagreeable thing that can be done to those of the best sense amongst his late friends, is to *make mention of his name,* and that, therefore, there is no doubt that the justice and the clemency of His Majesty's Government will in a very few years universally gain the hearts of men who already have got rid of that fascination that so lately blinded them.'

Slander had conquered.

III

THE YOUTH OF CHARLES

THE accession of the Second George dimmed the prospect of a speedy restoration. The Tories now stood well at Court. Their discontent with the Hanoverian dynasty was allayed. During the long period of deferred hope Charles and his younger brother Henry displayed in their childhood the graces and the charms that contrasted with the fetid atmosphere of the Hanoverian Court. The detractors of Charles find in gossip about his wilfulness the first signs of the wilfulness they attribute to his character in maturity. Yet the tales are those that might have been related of any high-spirited boy, and they lack importance. The portrait of him at seven and a half drawn by the Duke of Liria is attractive enough. The Prince of Wales according to his cousin was remarkable for beauty, grace, and cleverness. He could read fluently, and knew the doctrines

16

of the Christian faith. He could ride, he could fire a gun with a good aim and split a rolling ball with a cross-bow ten times in succession. He spoke English, French, and Italian perfectly, and was the most ideal Prince the Duke had met.

The first great experience of his life was when he was allowed at the age of fourteen to go to the siege of Gaeta, where the Duke of Liria, presently to become Duke of Berwick in succession to his gallant father, had a command under Don Carlos against the Austrians.

Greatly excited, Charles set out in July 1734, accompanied among others by his tutors the Protestant Lord Dunbar and the Catholic Sir Thomas Sheridan. Pope Clement XII. had given him his blessing and a good tip, and when he arrived on the field of action he was received by Don Carlos with great friendliness and respect. The royal boy had a splendid time, especially with the rank and file of the army, with whom he was immensely popular. He behaved well under fire, and worried the Duke of Berwick by the way he would expose himself to danger. It was a relief when Gaeta fell and his young cousin was able to enjoy himself

17

among the soldiers without the risk of getting a bullet through him. Don Carlos invited the Prince to take part in the Spanish campaign in Sicily; but by this time his father thought he should return home and not risk his life any longer. Moreover, Queen Clementina was now seriously ill, and in January 1735 she died.

There is little to glean about the relations between Charles and his mother. A few tender and pious little notes from her to him have been preserved, and in a letter from Charles to his father, written when he was about eight, we have a hint of the Queen's nervous condition:

'DEAR PAPA,—I thank you mightily for your kind letter. I shall strive to obey you in all things. I will be very dutiful to Mamma, and not jump too near her. I shall be much obliged to the Cardinal for his animals. I long to see you soon and in good health.—I am, dear Papa, your most dutifull and affectionate Son,   CHARLES P.'

An echo of laughter from a fair brown-eyed boy is heard across the years, and with it mingles the sigh of a disappointed Queen. Yet hers was the Polish fire that gave him such ardour of action, and when she lay dying he was ill with grief.

In 1737, after two years of quiet study, with plenty of golf and hunting, during which he made himself proficient in music and learnt to play the violoncello, the Prince, under the title of Count Albany, made a tour of the Italian cities with Dunbar and Sheridan. The progress was a triumph, so notable a triumph indeed that the various envoys of the Second George protested formally against the attention that was being paid to his young rival. The reception he was accorded in Venice so much angered the Elector that the Venetian Resident in London was expelled. Charles enjoyed his royal progress; but his mind was concentrated upon deeds, and he would be taking long walks barefooted over the Italian hills to prepare his body for the enterprise to which already he had pledged his life.

IV

THE CALL OF SCOTLAND

EVEN as early as 1738 Charles had broached the idea of trying his fortunes in Scotland; but the King had refused his permission, and for the next seven years the Prince brooded over his project. It was natural that Charles should look to the Highlands of Scotland to give him back the throne for his father. There were memories of Montrose and Dundee. The bugbear of Popery had no terrors for a country that was still predominantly Catholic in outlook, although in many districts the practice of their religion was denied to the clans by the enforcement of penal laws. Even those clans that were not Roman Catholic were Episcopalian, with a still profounder hatred of Presbyterianism and Whiggery. Only in the extreme north and north-east, among the Mackays, Rosses, and Munros, or in the south-west among the Campbells, had Presbyterianism penetrated, and there as a political expedient but not, so far, as a spiritual force.

The Disarming Act passed after the Rising of 1715 had been a farce, because the only clans that had surrendered their arms were the so-called 'loyal' clans. General Wade's roads, for which his memory is so much honoured, were resented by the people through whose land they passed. The benefits they were supposed to confer were as yet imperceptible, and their chief effect in the eyes of the Highlanders themselves was to give mobility to the hated redcoats, and to spoil the feet of the cattle when they were being driven down to the southern markets. Poor General Wade was filled with as much consciousness of merit as Duncan Forbes himself. He believed that he was a civilizing force. Here is an extract from his report:

'Their notions of virtue and vice are very different from the more civilized part of Mankind. They think it a most Sublime Virtue to pay a Servile and Abject Obedience to the Commands of their Chieftains, altho' in opposition to their Sovereign and the Laws of the Kingdom, and to encourage this, their Fidelity, they are treated by their Chiefs with great Familiarity, they partake with them in their Diversions, and shake them by the Hand wherever they meet them.

'The Virtue next to this, in esteem amongst them, is the love they bear to that particular Branch of which they are a part, and in a Second Degree to the whole Clan, or Name, by assisting each other (right or wrong) against any other Clan with whom they are at Variance, and great Barbarities are often committed by One, to revenge the Quarrels of Another. They have still a more extensive adherence one to another as Highlanders in opposition to the People who inhabit the Low Countries, whom they hold in the utmost Contempt, imagining them inferior to themselves in Courage, Resolution, and the use of Arms, and accuse them of being Proud, Avaricious, and Breakers of their Word. They have also a Tradition amongst them that the Lowlands were in Ancient Times, the Inheritance of their Ancestors, and therefore believe they have a right to commit Depredations, whenever it is in their power to put them in Execution.'

To King James the Highlanders looked, not as King of Great Britain but as King of Scots, to restore to them the Scotland that was rightfully theirs. Whatever manner of unpleasant creature a Whig might have been, the fact that he opposed the rightful Chief of Chiefs would have been sufficient to rouse the antagonism of the Highlander. But, beyond political considerations, to the Gael a Whig was the expression of a diabolic materialism. Mrs. Grant of Laggan, writing early in the nineteenth century, said that for a Highlander

'Whig was an appellation of comprehensive reproach . . . it was used to designate a character made up of negatives: One who had neither ear for music, nor taste for poetry; no pride of ancestry; no heart for attachment; no soul for honour. One who merely studied comfort and conveniency, and was more anxious for the absence of positive evil than the presence of relative good. A Whig, in short, was what all highlanders cordially hated,— a cold, selfish, formal character.'

It was to destroy Whiggery that Prince Charles was born. From the moment of his birth the Gaelic poets had been proclaiming his advent as the saviour of his people, and without a knowledge of the Gaelic poetry and songs of this period it is impossible to understand the great longing that the arrival of the Prince appeased.

Almost every biographer of Charles has failed to appreciate the legend of the deliverer which for years had possessed the Gaels with a fervour of Messianic belief.

When Charles landed in Scotland he was not

gratifying an impulse of vanity or displaying an unimaginative selfishness. He believed that it was as much his duty as he knew it was his desire to take the course of action he did.

V

THE CALL HEARD AND ANSWERED

In October 1740 the Emperor Charles VI. died, and not long after Maria Theresa had ascended the throne of Hungary Europe was at war again, with the usual prospect of finding France and England on different sides. Men of influence in Scotland, Wales and England began once more seriously to contemplate the possibility of a Stuart restoration, which would put an end to what was held to be the disastrous continental policy of a still insecurely and resentfully united Kingdom.

James was not well served by Sempill and Balhaldie, his agents in Paris for affairs in Scotland; but he had found a most capable Scottish representative in John Murray of Broughton. To make intelligible the intrigues, cabals, and secret missions of these years would require more space than a short biography like this can afford. Matters hung fire for a couple of years,

and Murray's own account of the endless nego-
tiations definitely to commit the Scottish leaders
either to drawing their swords from the scab-
bards or the silver from their purses is a revela-
tion of human pettiness and indecision.

In January 1743, Cardinal de Tencin succeeded Cardinal Fleury as the chief director of
French policy. In June 1743, as a result of
the provocative action of the English in sending
troops to Flanders the year before, the battle
of Dettingen was fought, although technically
England and France were still at peace and
only fighting with one another as auxiliaries,
England and Hanover of the Queen of Hungary, France of the Elector of Bavaria, who had
been crowned Emperor as Charles VII. Louis xv.
was furious, and the new Minister, who had
several reasons to be personally grateful to King
James, was able to persuade His Most Christian
Majesty to invite Prince Charles to Paris and
sanction preparations for an invasion of England.

On January 9th, 1744, Charles left his bed
in the middle of the night, and with a few attendants rode northward through Italy to win
a kingdom for his father, being then just twenty-

four years old. Disguised first as a Neapolitan courier, he passed through Tuscany as an officer in the Spanish army to reach Genoa and Savona, whence under the name of Graham he sailed through the British fleet to land at Antibes and reach Paris on January 29th. From Paris he went in secrecy to Gravelines on the coast, where he waited in seclusion while the preparations for the invasion went forward at Dunkirk. Marshal Saxe was in command. A gale sprang up, and the fleet of French transports was irreparably damaged, several of them being wrecked off Dunkirk with the loss of every life on board. This calamity discouraged the French from proceeding with the invasion, and Marshal Saxe was given the command in Flanders.

The bitterness of Charles's disappointment when the storm wrecked the transports and dispersed the French fleet made him determined to rely henceforth upon himself. He actually proposed to hire a fishing boat and sail to Scotland alone, but on second thoughts invited the Earl Marischal to accompany him. Lord Marischal, however, had no taste for such adventures so many years after the fiasco of

1719, and he discouraged the Prince's project. Charles then proposed to join the French army in Flanders; but once again Lord Marischal dissuaded him on the grounds that he would do himself and the Cause no good by appearing in the field against his British subjects. It may be doubted if this was good advice. James III. had fought valiantly at Oudenarde and Malplaquet, and won so much admiration from the English troops that if he had ventured to cross over and put himself at their head they might have followed him and deposed 'brandy-faced' Anne. However, Lord Marischal never concerned himself to help Charles. He disliked him personally, and indeed had no love for any of the Stuarts. His political ideal was a Scottish republic separated from the English Crown.

So Charles, thwarted of the action for which his heart craved, returned to Paris, where he had lived with a young banker, Aeneas Macdonald, who was a brother of Donald Macdonald of Kinlochmoidart. Although it had been at the direct suggestion of Louis xv. that Charles had left his father's Court in Rome, the French King would not even grant him an interview. We may be sure that the association with Aeneas Macdonald strengthened the Prince's resolve to try his fortunes in Scotland at the earliest possible moment. We may be equally sure that the two poems of Alexander Macdonald, greatest of modern Gaelic poets, which were translated to the Prince by his host, played a great part in encouraging him to put his whole trust in the clans by the pledge they gave him of the response fidelity would make to faith. It is significant that not even the Campbells are omitted from the list of clans who the poet prophesies will hasten to join the Prince when he lands from overseas.

The year 1744 wore away in an atmosphere of petty intrigue; but thanks chiefly to the energy and devotion of John Murray of Broughton a kind of effort was made in Scotland to organize seriously the preparations for a Jacobite rising when the Prince should land. Sir Thomas Sheridan had been sent from Rome to join his old pupil, and as secretary the Prince had the services of the Rev. George Kelly, who had suffered fourteen years' imprisonment for the Cause. Sheridan and Kelly both supported Murray of Broughton in trying to counteract the bad advice of Balhaldie and Sempill, whose

incompetency, lies, and braggadocio were bane-
ful. It was during these months, while Charles
was being bamboozled—a word that was to become a favourite of his one sad day—and kept
'fooling around,' as no doubt he would have
called it now, that Lancashire legend declares
he made a secret journey to England and was a
guest of Sir Oswald Mosley at Ancoats Hall near
Manchester. The story may be true. There
were already moments when the atmosphere of
jealousy and intrigue in Paris stifled him.

Early in 1745 much plotting was toward in
Edinburgh, where secret meetings were being
held in a tavern under the piazza of Parliament
Close. Prominent at these meetings was Macleod of Macleod, a recreant when the moment
came, and Alasdair Macdonell, the younger, of
Glengarry, who held a captain's commission
under the French King in the Scots Brigade,
but a traitor too at last. Prominent was Lord
Traquair, half fool, half knave. Indeed of all
the conspirators only Donald Cameron, the
younger, of Lochiel and the Duke of Perth were
to command enduring respect. The Duke of
Perth believed that if the English Jacobites were
earnest in their sentiments there would be no

reason to call on foreign help; but all the others insisted that there was no chance of a successful rising in Scotland without foreign help. Murray of Broughton worked on indefatigably, risking arrest and death, and at last Macleod gave him a letter to say that he, who had truly considered His Royal Highness's resolution, was of opinion that to land in Scotland without assistance from abroad might prove an unsuccessful attempt, but that if he should land he would join him at the head of his clan. He preferred dishonour when the hour came. In June 1745, Sir Hector Maclean visited Scotland to clear up some wretched squabble. He was denounced and arrested in the Canongate of Edinburgh for high treason. This was a calamity, for without their Chief the Macleans could hardly be counted upon. Moreover, if Sir Hector had not been arrested, Macleod might not have gone back upon his word. Sir Hector, who had already suspected his honour, intended on this visit to hold Macleod to his word or force him to fight a duel, which it was generally believed Macleod would have shirked.

Meanwhile, Charles in France had grown sick of talk. When in May the French under

Marshal Saxe defeated at Fontenoy the British, Dutch, and Hanoverians under the Prince of Hanover, known as the Duke of Cumberland, he decided to act. In June, from the Château de Navarre where he was staying with the Duc de Bouillon, he wrote to his father in Rome:

'I am to tell you what will be a great surprise to you. I have been, above six months ago invited by our friends to go to Scotland, and carry what money and arms I could conveniently get; this being they are fully persuaded, the only way of restoring you to the crown, and them to their liberties. . . . After such scandalous usage as I have received from the French court, even had I not given my word to do so, or got so many encouragements from time to time as I have had, I should have been obliged, in honour and for my own reputation, to have flung myself into the hands of my friends, and die with them, rather than live longer in such a miserable way here, or be obliged to return to Rome, which would be just giving up all hopes. . . . Your Majesty cannot disapprove a son's following the example of his father. You yourself did the like in the year 1715; but the circumstances now are indeed very different, by being much more encouraging. . . . I have been obliged to steal off, without letting the king of France so much as suspect it. . . . Let what will happen, the stroke is struck, and *I have taken a firm resolution to conquer or to die, and to stand my ground as long as I shall have a man remaining with me.*

. . . Whatever happens unfortunate to me, cannot but be the strongest engagement to the French court to pursue your cause. Now, if I were sure they were capable of any sensation of this kind, if I did not succeed, I would perish, as Curtius did, to save my country and make it happy; it being an indispensable duty on me as far as lies in my power. . . . I write this from Navarre, but it will not be sent off till I am on shipboard. . . . I should think it proper (if your majesty pleases) to put myself at his holiness's feet, asking his blessing on this occasion; but what I chiefly ask is your own, which I hope will procure me that of God Almighty, upon my endeavours to serve you, my family, and my country.'

The resolution that this letter shows in words was confirmed in actions. The Prince borrowed money from Waters, a banker in Paris, and bought a large store of arms and ammunition in which were included twenty small field-pieces. Mr. Anthony Walsh, a wealthy Irish merchant of Nantes, agreed to take the Prince to the coast of Scotland in his armed brig, the *Du Teillay*[1]; and a countryman of his, Walter Rutledge, obtained letters of marque to cruise off the coast of Scotland with the French frigate *Elizabeth* of sixty-odd guns. Somehow or other,

[1] There seems no reason to persevere with a misspelling like *Doutelle.*

33

without the knowledge of the French Government, this ship was put at the Prince's disposal to carry his military stores and convoy the *Du Teillay*.

During these preparations the Prince and those who were to share in his enterprise lodged in different parts of the town of Nantes without entering into communication with one another. The Prince himself was disguised as a student of the Scots College in Paris under the name of Douglas. With him was his old tutor Sir Thomas Sheridan, then seventy years of age, the Rev. George Kelly, Captain O'Sullivan, an Irish soldier of fortune whose reputation as a man and a soldier was extremely high all over Europe, Sir John Macdonald, another Irish soldier of fortune of whom not much is known, Aeneas Macdonald the banker, Colonel Francis Strickland, a member of an old family of Westmorland Jacobites, who had acted as major-domo for King James in Rome but had somehow annoyed his Royal master, and finally, the attainted Duke of Atholl, a veteran of 1715 and 1719, over sixty years of age and crippled by rheumatism. Besides these there were several attendants, among whom was Duncan Cameron, a native of the island of Barra, who had been Old Lochiel's servant for a long time, and had been engaged as a pilot.

On the evening of June 22nd, the adventurers embarked on board the *Du Teillay* at Bonne Anse, about six kilometres from St. Nazaire, and proceeded to Belle Isle to await the arrival of the *Elizabeth*. Here was written the Prince's last letter to his father with date of July 12 (N.S.):

'After having waited a week here, not without a little anxiety, we have at last got the escort I expected, which is just arrived; namely, a ship of 68 guns, and 700 men aboard. I am, thank God, in perfect health, but have been a little sea-sick; and expect to be more so; but it does not keep me much a-bed, for I find the more I struggle against it the better.'

Charles had already notified Murray of Broughton that he was coming, and as often happens when talk ends and action begins, the talkers were dismayed. The bold conspirators of Edinburgh taverns sent Murray to hang about for a month on the west coast to intercept the Prince and beg him not to land. When he had not arrived by the end of June, Murray supposed that the project had been abandoned and went home to Peeblesshire.

On July 5th the *Du Teillay* and the *Elizabeth* sailed. Four days later when off the Lizard the *Lion*, an English frigate of seventy-four guns, met them and was engaged by the *Elizabeth*. The Prince was most anxious to bring the *Du Teillay* into the action, but Walsh threatened to order him below if he tried to interfere, and said the two frigates must fight it out alone. As usual, the Prince was right. The help of the *Du Teillay* might have made just the difference. As it was, the two ships were so badly damaged after a fight lasting over five hours that both had to put back to port. Captain Douaud [1] was killed and Captain Brett was seriously wounded.

After the loss of the convoy with so many military stores some of the Prince's companions urged him to return. This he refused to do, and on July 22nd the towering cliffs of Barra Head, the most southerly point of the Outer Hebrides, were sighted. The *Du Teillay* sailed on until off Barra, when Duncan Cameron went ashore in the longboat to find a proper

[1] Not d'Eau or d'O.

pilot. He fell in with the piper of Macneil,[1] who guided the *Du Teillay* to a safe harbourage on the west side of the small island of Eriskay which lies between Barra and South Uist.

The beach on which the Prince disembarked is an expanse of gleaming silver sand below a green slope which on that drizzling July day would have been powdered with the gold of lady's bedstraw. The rocks of Eriskay are uniformly grey, but in the low out-thrust where the Prince's foot first touched the land of his ancestors they are the colour of a faded bloodstain. Little is changed in the Eriskay of to-day from the island as it was in 1745. Standing by the wall of a thatched house may be seen the great-great-granddaughter of the man who carried the Prince ashore on his back. The big rosy convolvulus, the seeds of which he had gathered when waiting on the coast of France, still flowers on the spot where he dropped them, and only there in Eriskay or any other Hebridean island. Time has no power over Eriskay. What was is.

After spending a night in a cottage the Prince

[1] Tradition in Barra says that he brought the Prince 300 guineas from Macneil, who was himself away from the island.

sent a message to Alexander Macdonald of Boisdale at Kilbride in South Uist, which lies a couple of miles away across a stretch of water more richly coloured than a peacock's tail. Boisdale, who had already been warned by Sir Alexander Macdonald of Sleat that the Prince was likely to arrive and who knew that Sir Alexander intended to break his pledged word, did his best to persuade the Prince to go home.

'Home?' said Charles, 'I am come home.'

Although he could not prevail upon the Prince to falter in his purpose, Boisdale was successful in persuading his brother Clanranald to forbid the Macdonald islesmen to follow him. Aeneas Macdonald, however, took a boat and went ahead to Moidart, where he informed his brother Kinlochmoidart of the Prince's arrival and summoned various Clanranald chieftains to meet him.

On July 25th, the *Du Teillay* sailed from Eriskay across to the mainland and anchored in Loch nan Uamh, an inlet of the sea between Moidart and Arisaig. We possess a vivid account of the scene on board written by an anonymous Clanranald kinsman, who, the present writer is satisfied, is none other than the great Gaelic poet Alexander Macdonald.[1] He arrived on board with young Clanranald, Glenaladale, and his brother Dalilea. He writes:

'We called for the ships boat and were immediately carryed on board, and our hearts were overjoyed to find ourselves so near our long wished for Prince. We found a large tent erected with poles on the ships deck covered and well furnished with variety of wines and spirits . . . there entered the tent a tall youth of a most agreeable aspect in plain black coat with a plain shirt not very clean and a cambrick stock fixed with a plain silver buckle, a fair round wig out of the buckle, a plain hatt with a canvas string haveing one end fixed to one of his coat buttons; he had black stockins and brass buckles in his shoes; at his first appearance I found my heart swell to my very throat . . . he saluted none of us, and we only made a low bow at a distance. I chanced to be one of those who were standing when he came in, and he took his seat near me but immediately started up again and caused me sitt down by him upon a chest. I at this time taking him to be only a passenger or some clergyman, presumed to speak to him with too much familiarity yet still retained some suspicion

1 Lang asserts without any justification that the anonymous chronicle of the *Lockhart Papers* was written by Morar himself, and Blaikie says he was assured it was by young Ranald of Kinlochmoidart. The internal evidence that it was by the poet is incontrovertible.

39

he might be one of more note than he was said to
be. He asked me if I was not cold in that habite
(viz. the highland garb) I answered I was so ha-
bituated to it that I should rather be so if I was to
change my dress for any other. At this he laughed
heartily and next enquired how I lay with it at
night, which I explained to him; he said that my
wraping myself so closs in my plaid I would be un-
prepared for any sudden defence in the case of a
surprise. I answered that in such times of danger
or during a war we had a different method of use-
ing the plaid, that with one spring I could start to
my feet with drawn sword and cock'd pistol in my
hand without being in the least incumber'd with
my bedcloaths. Severall such questions he put
to me; then rising quickly from his seat he calls
for a dram, when the same person whisper'd me
a second time, to pledge the stranger but not to
drink to him, by which seasonable hint I was con-
firm'd in my suspicion who he was. Having taken
a glass of wine in his hand he drank to us all round,
and soon after left us.'

The Prince was successful in persuading
Young Clanranald to go to Skye and make an-
other attempt to rouse the recreant lairds of
Sleat and Dunvegan; Kinlochmoidart was sent
south to summon the Duke of Perth, Murray of
Broughton, and Cameron of Lochiel. On his
way across Loch Lochy he passed Bishop Hugh
Macdonald, the Vicar Apostolic of the High-

lands, and gave him the news of the Prince's landing. The Bishop expressed great nervousness about the consequences, and Kinlochmoidart shouted to him across the water, 'If the matter go wrong, then I'll certainly be hanged, for I am engaged already.' He foresaw his fate. Kinlochmoidart's services to the Prince as an intermediary were inestimable. He was captured in November at Lesmahagow through the agency of a divinity student. After being kept a prisoner in Edinburgh for nearly a year he was hanged, drawn, and quartered at Carlisle. The divinity student was rewarded with the living of Lesmahagow.

Bishop Hugh remonstrated with the Prince for not bringing any French troops, to which the Prince replied 'that he did not chuse to owe the restoration of his father to foreigners, but to his own friends, to whom he was now come to put it in their power to have the glory of that event, and as to returning to France, foreigners should never have it to say that he had thrown himself upon his friends, that they turned their backs upon him, and that he had been forced to return from them to foreign parts. In a word, if he could but get six stout trusty fellows to join him he would chuse far rather to sculk with them among the mountains in Scotland than to return to France.'

Presently Young Clanranald returned from Skye with news of the refusal of Sleat and Macleod to keep their words, and depressed by the result of his mission now tried to back out himself. Turning away from him, the Prince saw a youthful Highlander of some eighteen years standing by.

'Will you not assist me?' he asked.

The boy grasped his claymore, and cried, 'I will, I will, and though no other man in the Highlands should draw a sword I am ready to die for you.'

This was Ranald Macdonald, the youngest brother of Kinlochmoidart.

The next disappointment for the Prince was the arrival of Dr. Archibald Cameron with a message from his brother Lochiel beseeching the Prince to depart. However, Lochiel could not resist meeting Charles, and in the end he was persuaded to call out the Camerons. This loyal decision turned the day. None spoke now of holding back.

Charles, however, wisely decided by sending away the *Du Teillay* to anticipate any renewal of the suggestion that he should leave Scotland. With Walsh he sent a letter to his father, in which he wrote that if France declined to send help he was ready to die at the head of such brave people as he could find in Scotland. The poet gives a vivid picture of the Prince's effect upon his people:

'We did our best to give him a most hearty welcome to our country, the P. and all his company with a guard of about 100 men being all entertained in the house of Angus McDonald of Borradel in Arisaig in as hospitable a manner as the place could afford. H.R.H. being seated in a proper place had a full view of all our company, the whole neighbourhood without distinction of age or sex crouding in upon us to see the P. After we had all eaten plentifully and drunk chearfully, H.R.H. drunk the grace drink in English which most of us understood; when it came to my turn I presumed to distinguish myself by saying audibly in Erse (or highland language) *Deoch slainte an Righ:* H.R.H. understanding that I had drunk the King's health made me speak the words again in Erse and said that he could drink the King's health likewise in that language, repeating my words; and the company mentioning my skill in the highland

43

language, H.R.H. said I should be his master for that language.'

On August 11th Prince Charles sailed across to Moidart, where he was welcomed with violent enthusiasm by hundreds dancing a wild reel as he passed on his way to Kinlochmoidart House. Here he spent a week sending out summonses to rally to the Standard at Glenfinnan on August 19th.

Meanwhile, the Government had begun to move. On August 1st a proclamation had been published in the *London Gazette* offering £30,-000 to anybody that seized the Prince on his landing. On August 8th the news of the landing reached Sir John Cope in Edinburgh, who at once began to collect an army at Stirling. A few days later Lord President Forbes went to Inverness and rallied the Whig clans, raising twenty companies for Lord Loudon's Highland regiment.

Hostilities began when Macdonell of Tirnadris with some Keppoch and Glengarry Macdonells attacked two companies of Scots Royals who were marching from Fort Augustus to reinforce the garrison at Fort William, and took them prisoners. On August 18th Murray of

Broughton reached Kinlochmoidart, and the Prince was rowed up Loch Shiel to Glenaladale. a spacious green undulating country of surpassing loveliness. Here he was joined by Gordon of Glenbucket. The old man was sixty-nine and had been bedridden for three years. When he heard that the Prince had landed he felt 'a kind of new life,' and although bent nearly double, rode from Banffshire to the West, and then rode back again by September 5th to raise four hundred men.

At eleven o'clock on August 19th, the Prince, dressed in a dun-coloured coat, scarlet breeches and waistcoat, with a yellow bob at his hat, disembarked on the level ground at the head of Loch Shiel, expecting to find a Highland host, and found nobody. He was in despair. No doubt he was reassured then as he would be reassured now that time in the West Highlands is the servant of mankind. Anyway, after a while Macdonald of Morar arrived with 150 Clanranalds, and early in the afternoon the pipes of Lochiel's 700 Camerons were heard, and later on came Keppoch and his Macdonalds. The Stuart banner blessed by Bishop Hugh was unfurled and raised by the Duke of Atholl.

The white and crimson silk floated out upon an unanimous shout of welcome to the King of the Gaels. The Duke read out the King's Commission appointing Charles, Prince of Wales, to be sole Regent of his Kingdom of Scotland, England, and Ireland. The Prince replied with a brief but moving speech, and retired to his quarters in a small barn near by.

Major Macdonell of Tirnadris when lying under sentence of death used to say that he had never seen the Prince more cheerful at any time than when he had got together four or five hundred men about the Standard. Kinlochmoidart and Tirnadris, the two chieftains who did most to precipitate affairs, suffered death on the same St. Luke's Day at Carlisle, and from the dying speech of Tirnadris we may learn the inspiration of those who fought for Charles:

'I think myself obliged to acknowledge to the world that it was principle and a thorough conviction of its being my duty to God, my injured King and oppressed country, which engaged me to take up arms under the standard and magnanimous conduct of his royal highness, Charles, Prince of Wales, etc. It was always my strongest inclination as to worldly concerns to have our

46

ancient and only rightful royal family restored, and even (if God would) to lose my life chearfully in promoting the same. I solemnly declare I had no by-views in drawing my sword in that just and honourable cause, but the restoration of my king and prince to the throne, the recovery of our liberties to this unhappy island which has been so long loaded with usurpation, corruption, treachery and bribery; being sensible that nothing but the king's restoration could make our country flourish, all ranks and degrees of men happy, and free both Church and State from the many evil consequences of Revolution principles. . . . I here declare I die an unworthy member of the Roman Catholick Church, in the communion of which I have lived, however much her tenets be spoken against and misrepresented by many; and in that I now expect salvation through the sufferings and merits and mediation of my only Lord and Saviour Jesus Christ. But I hereby declare upon the word of a dying man that it was with no view to establish or force that religion upon this nation that made me join my Prince's standard, but purely owing to that duty and allegiance which was due to our only rightful, lawful and natural sovereign, had even he or his family been heathen, Mahometan, or Quaker.'

The man who spoke thus in his last hours was no romantic filibuster fascinated by the bright eyes of a Prince.

The arguments which at this date were being

employed at Inverness by Lord President
Forbes appealed only to the material interests
of those he sought to influence. His proselytes
were men like the cabbage-hearted Chief of the
Mackenzies and the double-faced Laird of
Macleod. His greatest feat of eloquence before
he succeeded in persuading so many Highland
gentlemen to play a coward's part was to persuade a jury to acquit of a rape Colonel Charteris, the vilest blackguard of the century. His
best admired attempts to solve the problem of
the Highlands seem to have been the suggestion
that Highlanders should be enlisted to fight in
England's wars of aggression, and his own agri-
cultural experiments on the fertile land of
Bunchrew. That he believed himself right is
at least as much a tribute to his vanity as a testi-
monial to his character.

It would be idle to pretend that material
motives never corrupted the Jacobite side.
Material motives were to enter as fast as they
always will when the success of any cause begins
to seem a possibility. Yet it may be claimed
that those who gathered round the Prince upon
that August day were almost to a man animated
by ideals and almost to a man unspotted by

worldly considerations. Jealousy had not begun to poison the atmosphere round the leader; suspicion had not begun to darken his own outlook. Success was at that date a mathematical impossibility, and the only victory was the victory of mind over matter.

To-day the figure of the Prince watches from the top of a baroque column erected by the piety of a later Macdonald of Glenaladale upon the green level at the head of Loch Shiel where he gathered his men that August day. The great west door of the Catholic chapel on the wooded slope above stands always open. Within, a brass tablet upon the white wall is inscribed *Charles Edward Stuart, R.I.P.* But lest his spirit should come again from the West the door is open for it; lest his spirit should come again to Scotland from Tir nan Òg, the Gaelic paradise of Eternal Youth beyond the ultimate West, the door is open.

VI

ADVANCE

ON the day the Standard was raised at Glenfinnan Sir John Cope left Edinburgh for Stirling, and against his own better judgment he
marched north to attack the Jacobite army.
Charles, whose generalship was infallible while
he was in undisputed command, hurried on to
take up a position on the Corriearrick where
he intended to offer battle with the advantage
of the position. On August 27th he put on the
kilt for the first time, and as he tied the laces of
his brogues he declared that he would be 'up
with Mr. Cope before they were unloosed.'
Charles was a match in powers of endurance
for any of his men. During the march on
Badenoch he lost the heel from one of his
brogues, and the men said they were glad of
it because he would be obliged to walk more
at leisure. He could run faster, jump higher,
and outwrestle them. He was even a better

man with the claymore in mock combats. Nor was it only physically that he strove to make himself one of his own men. He worked away at Gaelic under the guidance of Alexander Macdonald the poet, and throughout the marches he was hearing old tales of the Gaelic race and identifying himself with the mental outlook of his followers.

Sir John Cope was faced with the problem of advancing to the relief of Fort Augustus by Wade's road across the Corriearrick, and the more he thought about crossing a mountain pass where every coign of vantage would be held by the enemy, the less he liked it. His intelligence was valueless, as might be expected in a countryside so utterly out of sympathy with his object. His own men were deserting, and in the end he marched on in the direction of Inverness, leaving the road to the capital open for the Prince's army, which turned southward and reached Perth on September 4th, the Prince marching at the head of his men with a guinea in his pocket.

At Perth Charles was joined by the Duke of Perth, Lord Ogilvie, and Lord George Murray, the younger brother of the Duke of Atholl and

of Lord James, the Whig holder of the title.
Lord George was an able soldier, who had been
out in '15 and '19, but had been 'pardoned'
in 1724. The Prince at once appointed him
and the Duke of Perth Lieutenant-Generals
with Colonel O'Sullivan as Quartermaster-
General.

The relations between Lord George Murray
and the Prince provide the most controversial
matter in the history of the Rising. In their
anxiety to clear Lord George of the imputation
of treachery, in which most of the Highlanders
believed at the time, his partisans have not
scrupled to slander the Prince, and even smirch
the Cause. There is no ground whatever for
suspecting Lord George of treachery; but an
examination of all the evidence leads to the
conclusion that, whatever may have been the
personal virtues and within its limitations the
military ability of Lord George Murray, it was
his accession to the Cause which more than
any other single factor contributed most to its
ruin.

During the week at Perth steps were taken
to put the army on a footing and give it a more
soldierly appearance, to which Lord George

Murray's practical measures were of the greatest help. On the Sunday in Perth the Prince attended the service conducted by an Episcopalian clergyman, and thus early gave a practical example of religious toleration.

On the day the Prince reached Perth, Cope leaving Inverness had reached Nairn. On the day after the Prince marched south from Perth, he reached Aberdeen, whence he intended to move his army by sea to Leith and protect Edinburgh, which by now was in a state of hysterical alarm at the prospect of being attacked by a horde of savages. On September 13th the Prince's army reached the Forth, the opposite bank of which was occupied by Gardiner's Dragoons. There was some hesitation among a few of the Highland officers who were quitting familiar country for the Lowlands; but when they saw the dragoons galloping off in the direction of Stirling, and when the Prince himself plunged into the water first and led the way to the opposite bank, there was no longer any hesitation. The Rubicon was crossed.

Next day the Highland army moved eastward across the field of Bannockburn, the guns firing upon them from Stirling Castle. 'The dogs bark but dare not bite,' said the Prince as a cannon ball fell 'within twelve ells' of him. Gardiner's Dragoons, joined half-way by Hamilton's Dragoons, galloped in a series of panics to the other side of Edinburgh. From Corstorphine the Prince sent a summons to the Edinburgh magistrates demanding the surrender of the city. In the middle of the discussion about the answer to be returned, a man on a grey horse whom nobody recognized rode into the Lawnmarket where the volunteers were mustered and announced that he had seen the Highlanders on their way, 16,000 strong. This finished the volunteers. Four companies at once marched up to the Castle and surrendered their arms to General Guest, their example being followed by the various bodies of militia.

During the night of the 16th a civic deputation visited the Prince to plead for time, but were warned that if the city did not surrender forthwith the Prince would not be answerable for the consequences. The city fathers were trying to gain time for General Cope to land his troops at Dunbar and rescue Edinburgh.

That night the Prince sent a body of 900 men under Lochiel to blow up one of the gates and try to seize the city by a *coup de main,* but strongly enjoined upon Lochiel that he was to use no violence if it could possibly be avoided. One or two stratagems were tried without success. Lochiel was about to retire when a hackney-coach, which had taken out the last party of deputies to the Prince's camp, returned empty to go to its stables in the Canongate. The Netherbow port was opened for it to come out. Captain Ewan Macgregor rushed in followed by some of the Highlanders, and to quote Alexander Macdonald, 'Our people with drawn sword and target, with a hideous yell . . . marched quickly up street . . . and forced their way into the city guardhouse and took possession. The main body drew up in the Parliament Close, and guards were immediately placed at every gate of the city; and the inhabitants cannot in justice but acknowledge that the behaviour of our Highlanders was civil and innocent beyond what even their best could have expected.'

The Castle, which was garrisoned with regular troops, did not surrender. Between twelve and one o'clock of September 17th the heralds proclaimed James VIII. and Charles

Prince Regent at the Market Cross, and shortly afterwards the Prince, between the Duke of Perth and Lord Elcho, who, presumably as an investment, had joined him the night before, rode through the city to Holyrood House amid the cheers of the populace. On this occasion he wore a short tartan coat with the star of St. Andrew, red velvet breeches, and a gold-laced bonnet of blue velvet with a white satin cockade.

News came that Cope had landed at Dunbar.

'Has he, by G—d!' the Prince exclaimed in elation.

The Hanoverian General with 2500 troops was at hand, and by September 19th had taken up his position on Gladsmuir between the sea and the high road about mid-way between the villages of Cockenzie and Prestonpans, his front protected by a bog.

The Jacobite army moved out to give him battle, and while darkness was falling on the evening of the 20th bivouacked on the east side of the moor where the bog seemed more practicable.

VII

VICTORY

At a council of war it was decided to attack the enemy at break of day. Charles wrapped himself in his plaid and slept in a field of cut pease along with his men. In the middle of the night a Mr. Anderson, who had been accustomed to shoot snipe over this ground, told Lord George Murray that he could show the army a path across the bog. The Prince and chief officers were roused from sleep. At three o'clock on the morning of Saturday, September 21st, the Jacobite army began to move in silence over the morass, and when the sun rose at six o'clock a thick mist still hid them, so that they were able to re-form after crossing the bog. There are several vivid accounts of the battle, but none more vivid than that of the Gaelic poet:

'We then marched chearfully on and engaged the enemy; . . . The enemys artillary plaid furi-

57

ously upon our left, especially on Lochiells battalions; their cannon also racked our right wing but did little execution. Their great guns were followed by a very regular fire of the dragoons on the right and left, and this again by closs platoons of all their infantry, which our men received with intrepidity and an huzza. . . . Our march up to the enemy till we came near was without pipe or drum, in the most profound silence till the attack was begun, when all our instruments tongues and hands were at work. . . . The P. left his guard on the march to the attack, talking earnestly to the Duke of Perth and Clanronald and giveing his last orders and injunctions; but returning to his guard, as I happened to pass near by him, he with a smile said to me in Erse, "Greas ort, greas ort," that is, "make haste, make haste." . . . At this time the enemys guard first perceived us, for we heard them call out "Who is there? Who is there? Cannons, cannons, get ready the cannons, cannoneers"; but our quick march and sudden and intrepid attack soon brought us into the midst of our enemys.'

The battle of Prestonpans was over in less than seven minutes. Five hundred of Cope's soldiers were killed, mostly by claymores, scythes, and Lochaber axes. The Highland losses were trifling. A thousand of Cope's soldiers were made prisoners, of whom nine hundred were wounded. It was an astounding victory of untrained ill-armed men over the veterans of

Dettingen and Fontenoy. Cope himself brought the news of his own defeat to Berwick at the head of his fugitive dragoons, the first time, as Lord Mark Kerr observed sardonically, that a general had been the first to arrive with the news of his own defeat.

Bloody though the massacre had been, the behaviour of the victors when the battle was over was most humane. The Prince himself cared personally for the wounded, and was much distressed. Immediately after the battle he sent word to the Presbyterian ministers in Edinburgh to request them to hold their public worship as usual. Nevertheless most of them left Edinburgh and made martyrs of themselves and their congregations by refusing to minister, the intention being to suggest the danger of religious persecution, although they held a written promise from the Prince that they were free to worship as they liked.

The Prince would not allow the victory to be celebrated by public rejoicings. On Monday, September 23rd, he caused this proclamation to be made:

'We, reflecting that, however glorious it may have been to us, and however beneficial to the nation in general, as the principal means, under God, for the recovery of their liberty; yet, in so far as it has been obtained by the effusion of the blood of his majesty's subjects, and has involved many unfortunate people in calamity, we hereby forbid any outward demonstrations of public joy; admonishing all true friends to their king and country to return thanks to God for his goodness towards them, as we hereby do for ourselves.'

The testimony to the outward graces of Charles is unanimous. If face and figure, if charm of manner and nobility of bearing could make a Prince, even the most rennet-blooded Whig might have hesitated to call him a Pretender. 'I don't believe Caesar was more engagingly form'd nor more dangerous to yᵉ Liberties of his Country than this Chap may be if he sets about it,' wrote a Whig lady, fascinated in spite of herself, at this date. Yet in the moment of victory all those outward graces appeared but to reflect a richer beauty of the mind and character. Generosity, courage, forbearance, chivalry, and compassion: these were his virtues. Was he not born to be King?

The wisdom of Charles in agreeing not to advance immediately into England was shown by the numerous additions to the strength of his forces throughout the next few weeks, mostly from Banff and Aberdeenshire and Angus. It might be argued that if the Prince had remained in Scotland, the history of the '45 might have been different. Such support as he received from the south of Scotland was given to him by those who hated the Union more than they loved the Stuarts. In a proclamation of October 17th he declared the 'pretended Union now at end.'

Many Scotsmen must regret that the Prince besides disavowing the Parliamentary Union did not attempt to make that severance final by separating the crowns. Even the alliance between Presbyterianism and Property might not then have managed to frighten the nation into the arms of England. As it was, the Prince had to decide that Scotland would be lost if England were not won. Even in Atholl the Duke was finding it difficult to raise his tenantry, and it was not until October 30th that he was able to join the Prince with 600 men.

That night a council of war was held to decide upon the route of the march south. The Prince wished to advance by Newcastle and attack Marshal Wade, who had just reached

61

there with tired troops, and whose 6000 Dutch-
men had been ruled out from fighting the
French and their allies by the capitulation of
Tournai. This would leave the two armies
equal. Lord George Murray argued that the
risk of battle should be avoided, and that the
advance southward should be made by way
of Carlisle to give the English and Welsh
Jacobites an opportunity to rise and join. The
council broke up without reaching a decision.
In the morning the Prince announced that,
although he still thought his own strategy was
right, in deference to the opinion of the majority he should no longer oppose the advance
by way of Carlisle. There is not space to set
out the arguments in detail; but Lord George
Murray was wrong and the Prince was right.
Lord George was a defeatist from the moment
he joined.

By November 1st Edinburgh was evacuated
except for a few wounded Highlanders, on
whom the soldiers of the garrison brutally re-
venged themselves. The Prince's army roughly
amounted to 5000 foot and 600 cavalry.

On November 10th Charles was demanding
the surrender of Carlisle within two hours;

but that night news came that Wade was marching to the relief of the town, which was exactly what Charles wanted to hear. The army was ordered to muster at daybreak to march and take up a position at Brampton, a hilly country suitable to the Highlanders. Unfortunately, Wade was not advancing, and the siege of Carlisle was resumed, the dispositions being skilfully made by Lord George Murray. Charles was still at Brampton when the white flag was hoisted, and sent Murray of Broughton to the Duke of Perth to arrange the terms of capitulation. This was resented by Lord George Murray, who wrote an exasperating letter to the Prince resigning his command. The resignation was accepted in a curt reply.

On Sunday, November 17th, the Prince, on a white charger preceded by a hundred pipers, rode into Carlisle. Lord George Murray, with the help of Elcho's poisonous tongue, had persuaded some of the leaders that the Duke of Perth's Catholicism would have a prejudicial effect on the English Jacobites, upon hearing which the always magnanimous Duke begged to resign his command. Murray of Broughton also asked the Prince to let him absent himself from the council rather than annoy his temperamental namesake, and in the end Charles was prevailed upon to reinstate Lord George Murray as sole second-in-command to himself. We are far now from Moidart. Yet the old spirit was in the rank and file. Lord George, after sulking through a council of war, had to admit when appealed to by the Prince for his opinion, that the army would follow him without hesitation, and the march was resumed, along roads now deep in the first snows of winter. Good tidings had come from the north. The fiery cross had been sent through Stratherrick and the Aird, and 700 Frasers with white cockades and sprigs of yew were drilling on the green in front of Castle Downie. But English and Welsh Jacobites were scarce indeed, though three or four joined the Prince at Preston, where for the first time the church bells rang out to welcome him. Southward still. Manchester was taken by a sergeant, a drummer, and a wh–re, who arrived in advance of the main army and beat up a couple of hundred recruits for the Prince.

On Sunday, December 1st, the Jacobite army evacuated Manchester, and part of it led by the

Prince forded the river above Stockport. An observer notes that the water 'took him up to the middle,' and that 'he was dressed in a light plaid belted about with a blue sash; he wore a grey wig, with a blue bonnet and a white rose in it.'

When Charles stepped ashore in Cheshire he found a small party of gentlemen to meet him with Mrs. Skyring. Her father had fought for Charles I. during the Great Rebellion. She herself as a small child had seen Charles II. land at Dover for the glorious Restoration. Ever since the Stuarts had been exiled she had sent half her income every year anonymously to the Kings over the water. On hearing that Charles had landed she had sold all her jewels and plate, and was come to offer the money to her Prince. 'Lord, now lettest Thou Thy servant depart in peace,' she murmured as she kissed the Prince's hand. A few days afterwards the old lady heard the news of the retreat from Derby and died of grief, aged nearly ninety years. Moidart is near again.

At Macclesfield news reached the Prince that the Duke of Cumberland had taken command of Ligonier's army, and that his cavalry were at Newcastle-under-Lyme, only seventeen miles away. A council of war was held, at which it was decided to make forced marches in order to get past Cumberland's army and advance as swiftly as possible on London. Lord George Murray was 'one of the keenest' for this measure. An opportunity to show off his military skill always brought out the best in him, and the way he outmanœuvred Cumberland on this occasion was masterly.

VIII

RETREAT

ON the evening of Wednesday, December 4th, the Prince entered Derby after a march of twenty-six miles. He retired to bed at once, worn out, to sleep what was to be the last happy sleep of his life. He woke next morning in high spirits, unaware that the courage of his leading officers had evaporated. In the words of Hay:

'Charles was just going out, and had put on his bonnet, when Lord George Murray came in and said to him that it was high time to think what they were to do; Charles asked him what he meant, as he thought it was resolved to march on. Lord George said that most of the chiefs were of a different opinion, and thought they should march back to Ashbourn and join the army from Scotland, which was believed to be following them fast.'

This army from Scotland was the 800 men of Lord John Drummond who had landed at Montrose, Stonehaven, and Peterhead. They consisted of his own French regiment of Royal

Scots, and 300 men from the French Irish
regiments. Two of his transports had been
captured by English ships. Actually this army
was not marching south at all, but it was used
as an excuse to justify the retreat in the eyes of
the rank and file of the Prince's army.

The whole of that Thursday was spent 'in
brigue and cabal.' The arguments produced
by Lord George Murray and the chiefs in
favour of retreat were the failure of the English
and the Welsh Jacobites to rise, the unwilling-
ness of the French to send substantial help, and
the certainty of having to fight in turn the army
of 30,000 which was gathered at Finchley to
defend the capital, Cumberland's army of
Flanders veterans,[1] 12,000 strong, now at Lich-
field, and Wade's army now at Wetherby.
Superficially, these arguments were trenchant.

Yet it can hardly be doubted that if Charles
had had his way he would have won the throne
for his father, and what is more, kept it. When
on that fatal Friday caution prevailed, the
situation was all in favour of audacity. First

[1] There is reason to suppose that even the Flanders veterans
would have turned against the reigning dynasty. A soldier
in Sinclair's Regiment had received a thousand lashes at
Pontefract on October 26th for drinking the Prince's health
and declaring that half the regiment would join him.

and foremost the Prince's army was in magnificent fettle. The rank and file were prepared to fight any number of Englishmen with complete confidence. The great army at Finchley was in fact a drunken rabble communicating their spirit to the footguards. In order to induce men to enlist to defend the dynasty the Government was offering a bonus of £6 to every man who would do so. The City was in a panic. There was a run on the banks, which were paying out in red-hot sixpences to gain time. The walls were plastered with Jacobite proclamations. £10,000 in sterling had been collected for Charles. Even George himself, who with all his detestable qualities did possess physical courage, was contemplating flight. Two days after the army left Derby an envoy arrived from Sir Watkin Williams-Wynn to announce that the Welsh Jacobites would rise at once. The Prince's leaders did not appreciate the fact that nothing succeeds like success. They misunderstood the apparent apathy of the welcome the Prince received in England. Charles II. had received an equally apathetic welcome on his way to Worcester. The English have always had a particular prejudice in favour of being on the winning side.

The history of the world was changed by the fatal decision of that December day. There is no doubt that James III. intended to abdicate in favour of his son, who would have made an ideal King. The American colonies would never have been lost. The French Revolution might never have happened, for it is not outside possibility that Charles would have become in fact as he still was in theory King of France too. The long martyrdom of Ireland would have been averted. The decline of Scotland into a provincial appendage would have been avoided. Religious toleration would have been achieved long before it was. There might have been no exploitation of the poor by cynical industrialism. But let speculation cease.

Lord George Murray, anxious to show that he could handle a retreat as capably as an advance, took command of the rearguard and bent his wits on outmanœuvring Cumberland for a second time. As for the Prince, his heart was broken. 'He who had marched on foot at the head of the men all the way was obliged to get on horseback, for he could not walk and could hardly stand.' And if the heart of the Prince was broken, so were the hearts of his men. Alexander Macdonald writes:

'. . . would to God we had pushed on tho' we had been all cutt to pieces, when we were in a condition for fighting and doing honour to our noble P. and the glorious cause we had taken in hand.'

The forces of materialism by which the Jacobite army had been deflected from their purpose found a symbol in the gross body and mind of the twenty-four-year-old Duke of Cumberland. Lord George Murray handled the retreat ably; but of course there were stragglers, of whom Cumberland wrote to the Duke of Newcastle, 'as they have so many of our prisoners on their hands I did not care to put them to death, but I have encouraged the country people to do it.' The English rustics, eager to show their enthusiasm for the winning side, butchered these sick stragglers who fell into their hands. Yet, not even the bitterness of retreat soured the Prince's mercy. Even spies were not hanged.

By December 13th the army had reached Lancaster, where the Prince insisted on halting a day to show that he would fight if attacked, and that his retreat was not a rout. This was the first sign Charles had given since that fatal Friday at Derby of a hope that perhaps even yet the Cause was not lost. Lord George Murray found a favourable position for the army to give battle, but perhaps just for that very reason the Prince changed his mind, and the retreat continued. Cumberland's cavalry, which had been joined by Wade's cavalry under General Oglethorpe, were in pursuit, and at the skirmish of Clifton some dragoons attacked the rear-guard, but were beaten off. This was a brilliant little action for which the chief credit was Lord George Murray's, and Cumberland himself was sufficiently discouraged to remain at Penrith till all his forces joined him.

At Carlisle the Prince found letters from Lord Strathallan with an encouraging account of the army at Perth, and from Lord John Drummond to say that he had brought over enough men and artillery to reduce the Scottish fortresses, and that the French were sending over a strong force shortly. Charles had already sent orders to Drummond and Strathallan to join him, and he undoubtedly expected them to do so very shortly. This was the reason for leaving the garrison in Carlisle, for which service the Manchester regiment, who were as unwilling to go to Scotland as the Scots were to remain in England, volunteered. Lord George Murray, three weeks later, ungenerously reproached the Prince for this, but elsewhere he says, 'I do not know who advised leaving a garrison at Carlisle. I had been so much fatigued for some days before, that I was little at the Prince's quarters that day, but I found he was determined in the thing.'

The treatment of the garrison after it surrendered was ferocious. 'I wish I could have blooded the soldiers with these villains,' Cumberland wrote to Newcastle, 'but it would have cost us many a brave fellow, and it comes to the same end, as they have no sort of claim to the King's mercy, and I sincerely hope they will meet with none.' They did not. Most of the officers were hanged and disembowelled alive on Kennington Common. By the nobility of their bearing they awed to silence even the gin-sodden London mob.

On December 20th, the Prince's twenty-fifth birthday, his men, who for six weeks had performed miracles of audacity and endurance in England, forded the swollen Esk and stood with their feet in Scotland again. Cumberland had returned to London and handed over his command to General Hawley, who reached Edinburgh with a well-equipped army of at least 8000 men about the same time as the Prince reached Stirling. Hawley, confident of victory, made it his first task to erect gibbets for the prisoners he proposed to take.

Stirling capitulated to the Prince on January 8th, and for two days the army was drawn up in line of battle at Bannockburn, awaiting Hawley's attack. When this did not materialize, the Prince, leaving 1200 men under the Duke of Perth to prosecute the siege of Stirling Castle, marched to Falkirk, and on the late afternoon of January 17th, in a storm of wind and rain which drove from the south-west into the faces of the advancing Hanoverians, the Jacobites were victorious. Hawley left about 400 men wounded upon the field with all his baggage, tents, guns and ammunition, and himself fell back on Edinburgh. Unfortunately this victory, which shocked and frightened the Hanoverian Government far more than Pres-

tonpans, was not followed up. The defeatist
element was daily gaining influence.

On January 6th Lord George Murray had
sent an intolerable letter to the Prince, demanding a permanent 'committee of commanders' to
give a majority decision in all military operations, reproaching the Prince for the sacrifice
of the Carlisle garrison, and using the retreat
from Derby as an example of the advantage of
a committee! Committees always have been
and still are the curse of Scotland, and here was
Charles, who had achieved the impossible by
his personality, invited to remit the Cause to
a committee. He replied with deadly logic:

'When I came into Scotland I knew well enough
what I was to expect from my Ennemies, but I
little foresaw what I meet with from my friends.
I came vested with all the Authority the King
cou'd give me, one chief part of which is the Command of his Armies, and now I am required to
give this up to fifteen or sixteen Persons, who may
afterwards depute five or seven of their own number to exercise it, for fear if they were six or eight
that I might myself pretend to the casting vote.
By the majority of these all things are to be determined, and nothing left to me but the honour of
being present at their debates. This I am told is
the method of all Armies and this I flatly deny, nor

do I believe it to be the Method of any one Army in the World. I am often hit in the teeth that this is an Army of Volunteers, and consequently very different from one composed of Mercenarys. What one would naturally expect from an Army whose chief Officers consist of Gentlemen of rank and fortune, and who came into it meerly upon Motives of Duty and Honour, is more zeal, more resolution and more good manners than in those that fight meerly for pay: but it can be no Army at all where there is no General, or which is the same thing no Obedience or deference paid to him. Every one knew before he engaged in the cause, what he was to expect in case it miscarried, and should have staid at home if he could not face Death in any shape: but can I myself hope for better usage? at least I am the only Person upon whose head a Price has been already set, and therefore I cannot indeed threaten at every other Word to throw down my Arms and make my Peace with the Government. I think I shew every day that I do not pretend to act without taking advice, and yours oftener than anybody's else, which I shall still continue to do, and you know that upon more occasions than one, I have given up my own opinion to that of others. I staid indeed a day at Lancaster without calling a Council, yet yrself proposed to stay another but I wonder much to see myself reproached with the loss of Carlile. Was there a possibility of carrying off the Cannon and baggage, or was there time to destroy them? and wou'd not the doing it have been a greater dishonour to our Arms? After all did not you yrself instead of proposing to abandon it, offer to stay with the Athol Brigade to defend it?

'I have insensibly made this answer much longer than I intended, and might yet add much more, but I choose to cut it short, and shall only tell you that my Authority may be taken from me by violence, but I shall never resign it like an Idiot.'

At the battle of Falkirk both the Prince and Lord George had played their parts well; but the disagreement between the two was not healed. A futile attempt to reduce Stirling Castle was undertaken by the French engineer commander, and three weeks were wasted upon it. Charles himself caught a severe cold after the battle and remained at Bannockburn House, where he was nursed by Clementina Walkinshaw, and where, perhaps, the fatal liaison between the two was begun.

On the day after Falkirk a gloom was shed upon the Highlanders by the accidental shooting of young Angus Macdonell of Glengarry by one of Keppoch's men. To the ominous effect of the unhappy affair was added the demoralization of inaction, and there were many desertions, chiefly from the Atholl contingent, many of whom had not been willing volunteers. It was proposed that the Prince should review the Highland regiments and restore the moral of the army, but he was persuaded not to risk his health. Lord George reviewed the men himself on January 27th, and wrote enthusiastically to his brother the Duke about their appearance.

Next day news came that Cumberland had left London to replace Hawley. Charles felt that the imminent battle would, in his own words, 'decide the fate of Scotland,' and the question was whether to await Cumberland on the field of Bannockburn or advance to meet him. Being always happier when he was advancing, Charles decided to go forward. He then sent word to Lord George Murray bidding him to remain at Falkirk, and making some suggestions for the battle he believed at hand. Lord George approved the plans with a few modifications, which he sent back on January 29th for the approbation of the Prince. The Prince's spirits, elated at the prospect of meeting Cumberland, were suddenly dashed. On the same day that Lord George approved the Prince's plans, and on the same day as he was writing to his wife to tell her he was expecting another battle in two or three days, he forwarded a memorial signed by himself and some of the Chiefs urging the Prince to retreat into the North, the chief reason given being the number of desertions.

The messenger reached Bannockburn early on the morning of January 30th, an ominous date already in Stuart history, and the date of Charles's own death forty-two years later.

'When Charles read this paper he struck his head against the wall till he staggered, and exclaimed most violently against Lord George Murray,' says Hay of Restalrig, who was an eyewitness. 'His words were, Good God! have I lived to see this?'

Presently the Prince pulled himself together and sent Sheridan to interview the Chiefs and take a letter setting out his own arguments in favour of awaiting the advance of Cumberland at Falkirk. Cluny and Keppoch came back at once with Sheridan to discuss the business personally. We have no details of that momentous interview; but we know that the arguments of Charles were unavailing, and the conclusion of the letter he sent back from Bannockburn to Falkirk that night is like the voice of doom:

'If you are resolved upon it I must yield; but

I take God to witness that it is with the greatest reluctance, and that I wash my hands of the fatal consequences which I foresee but cannot help.'

The chief argument used by the defeatist leaders in favour of retreat was the number of desertions, and the Glengarry regiment was cited in particular. It turned out that only ten of them had deserted. The desertions were chiefly from the Atholl contingent, of whose honour Lord George Murray was naturally and rightly jealous.

By retreating from Derby England and Wales were lost. By retreating from Falkirk Scotland was lost as well.

Owing to some confusion of orders, and a change of time which has never been cleared up, the retreat looked like turning into a disorderly rout. Cumberland reached Linlithgow on February 1st, so that the Prince's army only had fifteen miles start. On February 2nd Charles reached Crieff with the clans and most of the foot, and it was when he reviewed them that he found how grossly had been exaggerated the number of desertions. The council of war at Crieff was an angry one; but a decision was finally reached that the army should march in three columns northward. Lord George Murray with the Lowland regiments and the cavalry taking the coast road by Montrose and Aberdeen to Inverness, Lord Ogilvie's regiment and the Farquharsons moving north by Coupar-Angus to Speyside, and the Prince himself taking the clans back along the Highland road down which he had led them just five months ago.

Cumberland reached Perth on February 6th, and remained there to consolidate his subjection of mid-Scotland. At the end of the month he reached Aberdeen, and while waiting there until spring to prosecute the campaign he gave the countryside a foretaste of what was to happen after Culloden.

On February 20th Inverness Castle surrendered to the Prince, and to the delight of the Highlanders was blown up. The Prince's cold, from which he had never recovered after Falkirk, was made worse again by his adventure at Moy, when Lord Loudon and his Independent Companies of 1700 Highland pseudo-Whigs tried to capture him, only to be driven back in a panic by the blacksmith of Moy and

half-a-dozen Macintoshes. The Prince, however, had had to make a hurried escape from
bed when the alarm was raised. By the middle
of March he was seriously ill at Elgin with
pneumonia, and his condition caused grave
anxiety. At Elgin, too, John Murray of
Broughton, who had served him and the Cause
so faithfully and ably, fell sick, and his place
was taken, not at all successfully, by Hay of
Restalrig.

During these two months in which the Prince
held the country round Inverness he employed
the forces at his disposal with the greatest skill;
but the outlook was dark. The lack of money
was becoming serious, and just when money
would have been most useful a vital misfortune
happened. Back in the autumn the Jacobites
had captured off Montrose the *Hazard,* a sloop
of war which had been sent there to bombard
the town after Lord John Drummond's disem-
barkation. The prize had been rechristened
the *Prince Charles,* and had been sent to France
for money and supplies. On her way back she
was pursued by four English warships in the
Pentland Firth, and to escape them ran ashore
at Tongue. No worse place could have been

chosen, for on the other side of the bay was Lord Reay's house, and with him a number of Mackays from Lord Loudon's dispersed army. These set out to attack the French crew of the *Prince Charles* and captured them together with £12,000 and all the supplies. Lord Cromartie was despatched with a force of 1500 men to attempt to recover the treasure so desperately needed, and owing to this he and his men were not at Culloden.

In spite of illness and misfortune, the Prince kept up his spirits wonderfully. 'He appeared gayer even than usual,' says Maxwell of Kirkconnel. 'He gave frequent balls to the ladies of Inverness and danced himself, which he declined doing in Edinburgh in the midst of his grandeur and prosperity.'

IX

DEFEAT

At the beginning of April a cold and arid wind
from the east, symbolic of what Lord President
Forbes called common sense, swept the snow
from the hills and tamed the wintry torrents.
It was fit weather for marching again. The
dry rattle of the English drums was heard, and
the skirl of Campbell pipes false to the warm
westerly gales of home; and as Cumberland
marched from the east his supply ships followed
him with a favouring wind. The Jacobite army,
many detachments of which were scattered on
diverse operations, was hastily summoned to
muster for the last fight, and no doubt it was
the delay in gathering its full strength which
was the cause of the order given to the Duke of
Perth and Lord John Drummond not to dis-
pute Cumberland's passage of the Spey. It is
true that his artillery was probably strong
enough to cover the crossing, but Cumberland

himself wrote to Newcastle: 'It is a very lucky thing we had to deal with such an enemy, for it would be a most difficult undertaking to pass this river before an enemy who should know how to take advantage of the situation.'

The Jacobite intelligence was bad, and Cumberland's advance was much more rapid than the Prince and his officers had expected. The long delay in Aberdeen had created a false security. In Banff, at the instigation of the Presbyterians, Cumberland's troops had burnt an Episcopal chapel, and while clergymen in England and ministers in Scotland were preaching every Sunday from their pulpits that the Young Pretender and his bandits intended to deprive 'the pious public of their bibles,' the whole way through Aberdeenshire and Banff-shire bibles were burnt with prayer-books wherever they were found in chapel or private houses. So blows the east wind of common sense, and away over in Skye, Lord President Forbes with the recreant Laird of Macleod was practising an ignominious form of common sense by hiding in Dunvegan until the battle of common sense was won.

On Sunday, April 13th, the news reached

Inverness of Cumberland's rapid advance. The next day pipes and drums called the men to arms, and the Prince marched out of the town to Culloden House, the home of Lord President Forbes, which had been fixed upon as his head-quarters. Lochiel and his Camerons did not arrive from Achnacarry until the Monday evening, having marched over sixty miles in two days. That same night the Duke of Perth with the army of the Spey reached the camp. This hasty mustering completely upset the commissariat, for John Hay of Restalrig lacked the energy and ability of John Murray of Broughton to cope with an emergency.

Early on Tuesday morning, April 15th, the army was drawn up in line of battle on Culloden Moor. The choice of the actual site when a better one seemed to offer itself a mile or so away across the river Nairn is usually attributed to Colonel O'Sullivan; but the fact seems to be that the matter was thrashed out and that the first position was deliberately chosen to prevent Cumberland's slipping past and seizing Inverness, which would have put an end to any hope of revictualling the famished army.

The Prince found his men in good trim after

a night's rest despite their empty stomachs, and as he rode along the lines dressed in a tartan jacket and buff waistcoat saluting each regiment, the cheers were loud, rising to the pitch of fervour when some scouts came in with news of the enemy's approach. This turned out to be a false alarm, and it was learnt that Cumberland's men were celebrating the birthday of their fat young commander with rest, good food, and plenty of brandy.

It was resolved to attempt a nocturnal surprise and attack the enemy in camp while he was sleeping off the effects of the entertainment. It is not clear who first suggested this plan, but there was no dissentient voice. Even Lord George Murray was in favour of the project, and the Prince embraced him in his joy at this unwonted enthusiasm for a course of action after his own heart. The force was to advance in two divisions, the clan regiments and the Atholl brigade under Lord George Murray in the van, the Prince with the remainder in the rear. The march began about eight o'clock over a moorland track, and it was hoped to cover the ten miles before midnight. Unfortunately, the main body was unable to keep up with the clans, and Lord George Murray was continually having to send back messengers to ask what was detaining the others. At Kilravock the Duke of Perth rode on to tell Lord George that he must call a halt of a quarter of an hour for the rear column to catch up. It was now two o'clock, and there were still four miles to go. Hepburn of Keith and Anderson of Whitburgh, who had shown the way at Prestonpans, were with other officers in the van anxious to proceed; but Lochiel argued against going on, and Lord George Murray sided with those who counselled retreat. Here is an eye-witness's description of what followed:

'About two o'clock of the morning of the 16th the Duke of Perth came galloping up from aside to the front of the second line, and ordered the officers to wheel about and march back to Culloden. They had not gone above a hundred yards back when they met the Prince, who called out himself, "Where the devil are the men a-going?" It was answered, "We are ordered by the Duke of Perth to return to Culloden House." "Where is the Duke of Perth?" says the Prince; "call him here." Instantly the Duke came up, and the Prince, in an angry tone, asked what he meant by ordering the men back. The Duke answered that Lord George, with the first line, was gone three-quarters of an hour agoe. "Good God!" said the Prince, "what can be the matter? What does this mean? We are equal in number, and would have blown them to the devil. Pray, Perth, can't you call them back yet? Perhaps he is not gone far yet?" Upon which the Duke begg'd to speak with his royal highness. They went aside a very short space. The Prince returned and call'd out, "There is no help for it, my lads; march back to Culloden House." '

The famished army, worn out with the long all-night march over boggy ground, reached Culloden about six in the morning, and weary men were still straggling back at nine o'clock. Charles, who was as hungry and tired as anybody else, sent officers to Inverness to try by any means in their power to obtain provisions for the men, and then, having eaten a little bread and drunk some whisky, he flung himself down in his boots to sleep. His men slept anywhere, some so deeply that they were not woken by the noise of battle next morning.

Neither Charles nor any of his officers expected Cumberland to advance on that fatal Wednesday morning, April 16th. When the Prince was roused with the news that the Hanoverian army was close upon them, he was for the first time in favour of avoiding battle.

Yet most of the historians have accused him of insisting on fighting against the advice of his Scots officers.[1] No doubt, in the confusion caused by Cumberland's rapid advance, all sorts of plans were hastily discussed, and in the end a decision made to hold the ground and thus avoid, if possible, confusion worse confounded.

The rank and file of the Jacobite army, starved of food, exhausted by the night march, and drowsed with insufficient sleep, went to their positions for the last fight, five thousand of them against a well-equipped, well-fed, well-rested army about twice their number. Behind that army a black cloud of sleet and hail was coming up from the east to their support. In vain did eyes look for Cluny and his Macphersons, for Cromartie and his Mackenzies. Cluny was late, Cromartie had surrendered. Only three hundred Frasers under young Inverellachie, who was to be slaughtered in cold blood next morning when lying wounded, reinforced the dispirited Jacobites. As if for-

[1] Blaikie seems to consider that the official report of the Marquis d'Eguilles to the French King, preserved in the State Archives, decides the question against the Prince. The present writer, with a practical experience of official French reports during the late war, is not impressed by the value of the Marquis's evidence.

tune's malice were even yet not exhausted, it had been decided to place on the left the Macdonalds, who since the days of Bruce had claimed the right as theirs. For this Lord George Murray and possibly Lochiel were responsible.

'Our sweet-natured Prince,' says Alexander Macdonald, 'was prevailed on by L. and his faction to assign this honour to another on this fatal day, which right we judge they will not refuse to yield us back again next fighting day.'

With these words the poet brings his narrative to a conclusion, and it may be presumed that the Macdonalds did not charge at the first order, and that when they thought better of their rage it was too late.

The battle began with a cannonade on both sides, in which the superiority of Cumberland's artillery was terrible in its effect. There had been a proposal that Colonel Roy Stewart and his regiment should attempt to outflank the enemy and attack him in the rear, and for that reason the Jacobite troops were not ordered to charge at once. The Prince, in his anxiety to make the men stand firm, sat on his horse fully exposed to the cannonade, and the head of one of his grooms was taken off by a ball within a few yards of him.

At last, perceiving that it was hopeless to keep the men steady any longer, he sent an A.D.C. to give Lord George Murray the order to attack; but this officer was killed before he could deliver the message. Finally, Lord George himself sent word by Colonel Ker of Graden that the attack must be delivered at once. Ker received the Prince's orders and, noticing that the left wing was further away from the enemy than the right, he rode first across to the Duke of Perth, who was commanding there, before he gave the order to Lord George Murray and Lochiel on the right.

However, before either the right or the left could charge, the Macintoshes, whose first experience this was of battle with regular troops, charged from the centre without orders, led by Colonel Macgillivray of Dumnaglass. To avoid the fire of the cannon from the enemy's centre the Macintoshes swerved to the right, and this pushed the rest of the right too far in the same direction. Their flank had been covered by a stone dyke which had been regarded as a protection. Unfortunately, Lord George Murray had rejected a proposal to guard this specially, so that the Campbell militia were able to break it down and pour a deadly flanking fire into the advancing Jacobites. Yet, in spite of sleet and hail tearing into their faces, in spite of the enemy's steady fire, the Prince's right swept on, cut their way through two regiments, and flung themselves to death upon the bayonets of the second line.

The clans of the left-centre, owing to that right-hand swerve of the Macintoshes, had a much greater distance to cover before they were at grips with the English regiments. Moreover, there was now a wide gap between them and the right of the Macdonalds, who halted to allow reinforcements from the second line to fill this gap. The clans of the left-centre, after receiving a heavy fire from the Scots Royals and two English regiments, which they had returned with their muskets, were about to charge when they saw through a rift in the volumes of smoke all that was left of the right wing retiring. It was then that the left wing of the Jacobite army broke. Only Keppoch with a few Macdonalds and his nephew, Mackenzie of Torridon, charged forward to their deaths. The right and right-centre were almost annihilated. 'Lord George Murray behaved himself with great gallantry, lost his horse, his periwig and bonnet, was amongst the last that left the field, had several cuts with broadswords in his coat, and was covered with blood and dirt.' Maclachlans and Macleans, Camerons and Frasers were cut to pieces. Lochiel was wounded in both legs and carried off the field. Seventeen of the Stewarts of Appin were killed in saving the blue and yellow banner of their clan from the enemy. The Macintoshes were obliterated, with their yellow-haired commander Macgillivray. Another hero of Clan Chattan was Major Gillies Macbean who, when the Campbells broke down the stone dyke, flung himself into one of the gaps and cut down fourteen of the enemy before he was himself cut down.

Charles himself tried to persuade the second line to follow him in a last desperate charge; but the second line gave way when the red-coats advanced, though they did manage to check the pursuit of the first line by the dragoons. The Prince's army broke into two, one part flying along the open road toward

Inverness and the rest crossing the river Nairn and reaching the hills. Those who went to Inverness were pursued by dragoons and cut to pieces, and in the slaughter some of the inhabitants of Inverness who had come out to see the battle were included. A broad river of dead ran from Culloden almost to Inverness itself.

It was with great difficulty that the Prince was persuaded to leave the battlefield. Finally O'Sullivan had to turn the head of his horse and drag him away.

A bloody revenge was taken by Cumberland and his red-coats for the fright the Prince had given them and for the disgraces he had inflicted upon their arms. After the battle the wounded were massacred where they lay. Thirty or forty who had taken refuge in a barn were burnt alive. In the words of a red-coat himself, 'they were more like so many butchers than an army of Christian soldiers.'

It must be added that in carrying out the policy of terrorization which succeeded Culloden renegade Scots committed as many horrors as the English. The ravishing of pregnant women, the flogging to death of old men, the slaughter of infants, these were intervals of sport to relieve the monotony of laying waste the Highlands with fire and sword. It is impossible to find a single extenuating circumstance for the behaviour of the Hanoverian Government. An addition to an army order issued by Lord George Murray on the eve of the last battle was forged with Cumberland's connivance, in which Lord George was made to write, 'Give no quarter to the Elector's troops on any account whatsoever.'

Whiggery has always been willing to sacrifice honour for respectability.

X

THE WANDERER

THE intentions and even the movements of the Prince immediately after the fatal battle have been the cause of much controversy; but it seems clear enough that he had planned in the event of a check to retreat westward and rally his army at Fort Augustus. He never anticipated the overwhelming disaster that occurred. In the confusion caused by Cumberland's swift advance on the morning of April 16th, nothing was apparently settled about a rallying-point, and that the larger part of the survivors should have reached Badenoch seems to have been an accident.

The Prince rode westward away from the stricken field through Strathnairn, until at about eight o'clock that night he reached Gortuleg, a Fraser household in Stratherrick some ten miles east of Fort Augustus. In this house was Simon Lovat himself, who had spent the day in superintending the preparation of a large meal to celebrate the victory. The old man [1] was not daunted by the tidings of woe. He reminded the Prince of Robert Bruce, who lost eleven battles and won Scotland with a twelfth, and his voice may be heard in the letter written by Macleod of Muiravonside, the Prince's A.D.C., to Cluny Macpherson that night:

'DEAR SIR,—You have heard no doubt ere now of the ruffle we met with this forenoon. We have suffered a good deal; but hope we shall soon pay Cumberland in his own Coin. We are to review to-morrow, at Fort Augustus, the Frasers, Camerons, Stewarts, Clanronald's, and Keppoch's people. His R.H. expects your people will be with us at furthest Friday morning. Dispatch is the more necessary that his Highness has something in view which will make an ample amends for this day's ruffle.—I am, Dear Sir, Your's, etc.

'GORTULEG, *April* 16, 9 at night.

'We have sent an express to Lord Cromarty, Glengyle, and Barisdale, to join us by Bewly. For God's sake make haste to join us; and bring with you all the people can possibly be got together. Take care in particular of Lumisden and Sheridan,[2] as they carry with them the Sinews of War.'

[1] Nobody has suffered more at the hands of unctuous dullards than Lovat. He had great qualities.
[2] The nephew of Sir Thomas.

That this letter was sent to Cluny, who was Lovat's son-in-law, rather than to Lord George Murray is significant.

An hour or so after it was despatched there was an alarm of dragoons, and the Prince rode on past Fort Augustus to reach Invergarry Castle in the small hours of April 17th. There he waited until three in the afternoon, and then struck westward as far as Glen Pean. Word must have come to him that what was left of his army had mustered at Ruthven, so that at least two days would have to elapse before they could reach Fort Augustus. It is generally assumed that the contemptible letter which Lord George Murray wrote from Ruthven on April 17th did not reach the Prince before he arrived on the western seaboard; but why did he wait until five o'clock in the afternoon at Donald Cameron's house in Glen Pean before abruptly starting off across some of the fiercest country in Scotland to Glen Morar?

It seems probable that he took this step after receiving that letter from Lord George Murray which reproached him for ever raising the Standard, whined on for two or three pages about the incompetency of Hay and O'Sullivan,

99

and concluded by resigning his commission. In that case it would have been from Glen Pean that Charles sent the message for every man in Badenoch to fend for himself. He must have decided, after being blamed by Lord George Murray for not securing French help, that, cost what it might, he would obtain it now.

The Prince reached the west coast to find it beset by English ships. With him went Colonel O'Sullivan, Ned Burke, who was Muiravonside's servant, and Father Allan Macdonald. He was back in Arisaig whence he had started; but instead of staying at Borrodale House he took shelter among the wine-dark birch woods of Beasdale already shimmering with the first tenuous green of spring. Here he was joined by Young Clanranald and various gentlemen who had survived the disaster of Culloden, and here were held many discussions about the future. Clanranald wanted him to remain hidden in Arisaig; but Charles was determined to reach France and obtain help. Elcho accuses him of being afraid that the Scots intended to betray him as they had betrayed Charles I., and of course attributes this suspicion to the influence of the Irish officers. There is no time here to scratch the bites of vermin like Elcho. In the nervous strain that succeeded the wreck of his cause Charles may have turned for a time with relief to those who were not reproaching him or lamenting that they had ever followed his lead. Yet his intention to go to Skye and seek out the lairds of Sleat and Macleod does not argue any lack of faith in the Scots.

We may find in the meeting with Donald Macleod, that grand old seaman of nearly seventy years, the reaction of Charles against the jealousy of those in higher places and an expression of his confidence in the loyalty of humbler men. Donald Macleod of Gualtergill is indeed an Homeric figure, and from the moment that the Prince met him the narrative moves through a larger air. It was Donald who warned him against the madness of hoping for protection from Sleat or his own Chief, and who volunteered to procure a boat to take him to the Outer Islands.

As it happened, Charles would have done better to stay where he was, for hardly more than a week after he had risked his own life and the lives of the valiant crew by crossing on a night of storm from Borrodale to Benbecula, two

French ships, after beating off the attacks of three English ships, landed 40,000 louis d'ors at Borrodale itself, and sailed away next morning to France with the Duke of Perth, who died on shipboard, Lord John Drummond, Lord Elcho (of course!), old Sir Thomas Sheridan and others.

John Murray of Broughton, although miserably ill, did not leave with the others. He felt it was his duty to supervise the distribution and concealment of the treasure. In June he was captured at night in an exhausted condition by a party of dragoons, and when faced by death weakened and offered to give evidence against his own side. Bold men who stayed at home exhausted the vocabulary of invective to express their virtuous contempt for 'Mr. Evidence Murray.' His wife left him. He lived in misery to end his days in a mad-house. Yet many of those who were loudest in reviling him were themselves far baser traitors than he. His evidence brought no man to the block, not even old Simon Lovat himself. Murray was a Peter, but he was no Judas. The Prince, to whom he was always passionately loyal, was to visit him many years later in London, and with his for-

giveness bring him the only pleasure his unhappy future was to know. As for the treasure,
it was a curse, and the wretched squabbles over
it for the next seven or eight years were to in-
volve in equal disrepute many Highland gentlemen.

With the Prince sailed O'Sullivan, Captain
Felix O'Neil, a lovable Irish officer, Ned Burke,
Father Allan Macdonald, Donald Macleod, and
a crew of seven, among whom was Donald's
youngest son Murdock, who was a schoolboy in
Inverness and had played truant on the morning of the battle of Culloden in order to take
part in it, the worthy son of a noble sire. The
Prince left behind him a letter for the Chiefs in
which he explained his reasons for trying to
reach France as quickly as possible, and advised
them to consult with the Duke of Perth and
Lord George Murray over the best measures to
be taken until French help was obtained.

When after a fearful night of storm the boat
reached Rossinish in Benbecula on Sunday,
April 27th, word was sent to Old Clanranald
at Ormaclett on the west side of the island that
the Prince had landed. John Macaulay,[1] the

1 Grandfather of the Whig historian, Lord Macaulay.

Presbyterian minister of Barra and South Uist, refreshing himself in the house of a Papist after his Sabbath duties, sent off a spy who found out that the Prince intended to go to Stornoway in search of a ship. With the prospect of £30,000 and preferment the Reverend John sent word to his father the Reverend Aulay, minister of Tarbert in Harris, to warn the Reverend Colin Mackenzie, minister of Lochs in Lewis, and arrange for the capture of the Prince.

Presently Old Clanranald himself visited the Prince, and plans were made for him and his companions to reach Stornoway in the guise of a shipwrecked crew from the Orkneys. On April 29th, the storm having abated, they set sail, and the following morning reached the island of Scalpay off Harris, whence Donald Macleod was sent on to try to hire a vessel at Stornoway. The Reverend Aulay Macaulay, hoping to keep the reward in the family, made an attempt with some of his parishioners to seize the Prince; but they received such a discouraging reception from Donald Campbell, the tenant of Scalpay, that they retired.

News came that Donald Macleod had secured a ship, and the Prince with O'Sullivan, O'Neil,

and a guide sailed up Loch Seaforth, landed at
the head, and walked thirty-eight miles across
the wild Lewis moors on a dark night of driving
rain to within two miles of Stornoway, finding
shelter in the Catholic house of Mrs. Mackenzie
of Kildun. The inhabitants of Stornoway, having been told by the Reverend Colin Mackenzie
that the Prince was marching to attack them
with 500 men, gathered to prevent his reaching
the vessel, and even refused him a pilot to cross
over to Ross-shire and take refuge in the
Mackenzie country. Finally the Prince and his
companions had to retire, and after many
dangers and hardships, on May 14th reached
Corrodale in South Uist, whence Donald Macleod was sent to the mainland to try to get
some of the money which had arrived from
France. He was away for eighteen days and
was not successful.

During this time the Prince was well hidden.
He was able to rest, and not merely to rest but
to enjoy some sports, and he was visited by
various Macdonalds, most of whom were nomi-
nally serving in the Hanoverian militia. There
was a famous drinking bout one night, in the
course of which, during a discussion about re-

ligion and politics, the Prince insisted that most
of the rulers of Europe had little or no religion
at all. The discussion was ended by the Prince's
drinking all the others to the floor, when he
covered them up with their plaids and sang
'De Profundis' for the repose of their souls.
Among the roisterers was Macdonald of Boisdale, who was accounted 'as able a bowlman as
any in Scotland.'

By June 5th, hostile troops were closing in
and it was felt advisable to make a move, and
after being harried up and down the coast for
ten days the Prince reached Benbecula to find
that his friends were being arrested on suspicion
of harbouring him. It became imperative to
reach the mainland where there was more room
to hide, and it was now that Flora Macdonald's
help was invoked to get the Prince across to
Skye. Disguised as Betty Burke, an Irish serving maid, he reached Skye in safety on June
29th. The next evening Charles parted from
his rescuer at Portree.[1]

'I believe, madam,' he said, 'I owe you a
crown of borrowed money.' She told him it

[1] There was no sentimental attachment between Flora Macdonald and the Prince, though Captain O'Neil seems to have
fallen in love with her.

was only half a crown, which accordingly he paid her with thanks. He then saluted her, and expressed himself in these or like words, 'for all that has happened, I hope, madam, we shall meet in St. James's yet.'

The next devoted helper of the Prince was Macleod of Raasay, but Raasay being too small an island for safety, he went back with Captain Malcolm Macleod of Brea to Skye and reached the Mackinnon country, where the grand old chief insisted that he should have the honour of personally escorting him to the mainland. When he landed from Raasay the Prince had spent the night in a byre, and Boswell, years later, heard from Malcolm Macleod how restlessly the Prince had slept, and how between muttering broken phrases in English, French and Italian he would suddenly start and cry in his sleep, 'O God! poor Scotland!'

But deeper than despair lay the determination of the Prince to win at last. As he walked along in the guise of Malcolm Macleod's servant, he said to him:

'Macleod, do you not think that God Almighty has made this person of mine for doing some good yet? When I was in Italy, and din-

ing at the King's table, very often the sweat
would have been coming through my coat with
the heat of the climate; and now that I am in
a cold country, of a more piercing and trying
climate, and exposed to different kinds of
fatigues, I really find I agree equally with both.
I have had this philibeg on now for some days,
and I find I do as well with it as any the best
breeches I ever put on. I hope in God, Macleod, to walk the streets of London with it yet.'

With the old chief of Mackinnon and four
boatmen the Prince was rowed across to
Mallaig, where after hairbreadth escapes from
the militia he got into touch again with various
Macdonalds. Alas, 'the three or four thousand
bloody hounds, by sea and land, thirsting for
the captivity and noble blood of their Prince,'
were beginning to test the devotion even of the
faithful Macdonalds. Old Clanranald himself
declared he could do no more for the Prince,
and Macdonald of Morar said the same, much
to the indignation of the undaunted Laird of
Mackinnon. However, in the end Alexander
Macdonald of Glenaladale, whose house had
been burnt, whose cattle had been driven off
so that he could hardly support his wife and

five children, and who had been three times
wounded at Culloden, one of the wounds being
still unhealed, volunteered to serve his Prince
once more. As General Campbell with six warships full of troops anchored in Loch Nevis and
as the infernal Captain Caroline Scott occupied
all the lower part of Arisaig with troops,
Glenaladale himself, his brother John, and Iain
Òg, the son of Macdonald of Borrodale, in
whose house, now a blackened ruin, the Prince
had been welcomed just a year ago, set forth
with him to cross the 'rough bounds.'

On July 18th they reached Fraoch Bheinn,
from which the Prince could look down and see
far below the green head of Loch Shiel, where
eleven months ago within a day the Standard
had been raised. At dusk news came that a
hundred Campbells had reached the foot of
Fraoch Bheinn itself, so that they could not
wait for the arrival of Donald Cameron of Glen
Pean, who had been sent for to guide the Prince
out of infested Moidart. By the kindness of
fortune, at eleven o'clock that night they met
Cameron, who told them that there were
twenty-seven encampments of red-coats between
Kinlochiel and Kinloch-hourn, a distance of

only seventeen miles as the crow flies. Somehow they broke through the cordon and reached
Glenshiel, where the Prince spent a long wet
day hidden on a hill above Strath Cluanie and
was so tormented by midges that his companions
had to cover him with heather. He suffered
much from lice, and from an intermittent dysen-
tery, which makes his feats of physical endurance even more remarkable.

The next day the Prince joined the famous
seven men of Glenmoriston,[1] who had formed
themselves into 'a small association of offence
and defence against the Duke of Cumberland
and his army (he and the Laird of Grant having
betrayed so many of their countrymen upon
giving up their arms) never to yield but to die
on the spot, never to give up their arms, and
that for all the days of their lives.' The be-
trayal of the Grants of Glenmoriston and Glen-
urquhart by Ludovic Grant of Grant was as
vile an act as even a Whig ever perpetrated.
These seven superb figures of revenge had been
inflicting justice on any Highlanders who
helped the red-coats even as guides. Only a few

[1] Two Macdonalds, three Chisholms, a Macgregor, and a
Grant.

days before they had captured Robert Grant, a Strathspey man who had become notorious as an informer, shot him dead, cut off his head, and hung it from a tree on the high road three miles from Fort Augustus. To those men Glenaladale resolved to trust his Prince. The Prince was recognized at once by one of the seven, John Macdonald. 'At the sight of him,' says Iain Òg of Borrodale, 'the poor man changed colours, and turned as red as blood, and addressed him in the following manner, "I am sorry to see you in such a poor state, and hope if I live to see you yet in a better condition, as I have seen you before at the head of your army, upon the green of Glasgow: all I can do is to continue faithful to you while I live, and I am willing to leave my wife and children and follow you wherever you incline going." '

So with the seven men of Glenmoriston, who were presently to become eight by the arrival of Hugh Macmillan, the Prince stayed for a while in their cave of Corriegoe, and with them when Glenmoriston became too full of militia he wandered to Chisholm's country, hiding in Glen Cannich and in the woods of Fasnakyle, where he 'drank to the health of one of the daughters of the King of France, telling his companions that her hair was as black as the raven, and that she was a mighty fine agreeable lady, being sweet natured and humble, and that he, the Prince, could not fail to love her, as he was very sure that she entertained a very great regard for him, as did likewise the Dauphin whom the Prince commended much.' Thus relates Patrick Grant, one of the seven, and adds that they spoke about this lady for a whole hour without intermission.

On August 15th, by way of Glenmoriston and Glengarry, they came to Locharkaig, where they were joined by Macdonell of Lochgarry, who was optimistic enough to suggest the possibility of rallying the Highlanders to take their revenge. Word was sent to Lochiel and Cluny; but at the end of the month Lochgarry and Dr. Cameron came back from Badenoch to say that neither Lochiel nor Cluny believed a rally was possible now. They offered instead to conduct the Prince to Cluny's cage on Ben Alder. He parted from Patrick Grant, the last of his faithful band, whom he had kept in the hope of rewarding him. Thanks to the money brought by Lochgarry, he was able to give him twenty-four guineas.

On September 5th the Prince reached Cluny's cage, in which 'romantic comical habitation' he remained until news came of the arrival of two French ships in Loch nan Uamh. On September 13th the Prince with Lochiel, Cluny, Lochgarry, Dr. Cameron, and others set out from Badenoch to Moidart, and were joined on the way by Colonel John Roy Stewart, the soldier-poet and a great favourite of the Prince, who used to call him 'the Body.' To surprise him the Prince wrapped himself up in a plaid, from which he peeped out as John Roy was coming into the hut, in the door of which was a puddle of water. John Roy was so completely surprised that he cried out, 'O Lord, my master!' and fell down in the puddle in a faint.

On September 19th the Prince and a large number of followers embarked upon *L'Heureux* in the same sea-loch where fourteen months ago he had landed to try for a kingdom. In his heart he did not believe that the separation would be for long. He would soon return, and with this intention in his mind he asked Cluny Macpherson to remain behind in Scotland 'as the only person in whom he could repose the greatest confidence.'

So, when in the evening the Prince embarked for France, Cluny turned back to Badenoch and began that ordeal of eight weary years waiting for the Prince 'to pay him a visit soon in a way better supported than formerly.'

XI

HOPE AND DESPAIR

CHARLES landed at Roscoff in Brittany, his whole being actuated by one purpose, which was to return to Scotland and win. Away back in Glenmoriston and Strathglass Charles had been wont to speak with great affection of his brother the Duke of York, and Patrick Grant noted that 'he used to say much in praise of Prince Henry as one preferable to himself in all respects, and one of great spirits and activity.'

Yet, while Charles was thus praising his brother, King James was worrying himself about the future of their relationship. At the end of July he had written to the Duke of York from Rome, 'for God's sake, dear child, be on your guard, and whatever the Prince may happen to do or say that might be disagreeable to you, bear and suffer anything with as cheerful an air towards him as you can . . . you may be sure I will not suffer you should be oppressed.'

It is clear from such a letter that poisoned tongues had already been at work in Rome and elsewhere. Elcho had been squirting his venom and making things more than ever impossible for poor old Sir Thomas Sheridan, whom the King had always disliked. No sooner did Charles land than the atmosphere of jealousy and intrigue and backstairs gossip closed in upon him.

The Royal brothers met with an affection that was certainly sincere on Charles's side; but it is unpleasant to find the Duke of York writing to his father at the end of October, 'the Prince's love towards the Duke (himself) is undoubted and great, but that is all. All the click and their dependance have sway and no one else.'

Charles had always hated the King's favourites like Balhaldie and Sempill, and the King had hated his son's equally—poor George Kelly, good old Sir Thomas Sheridan, and Colonel Strickland who had died as a prisoner in Carlisle. He was not blind to the jealousy of the Duke of York over the popularity of the returned hero in France. After his first interview with Louis xv. he wrote to the King, 'the reason why I did not speak to Your Majesty

about my affairs last night was because my
brother was present, and, loving him tenderly,
I was anxious to avoid giving him cause for
jealousy.' Charles then begged Louis to give
him a private audience. The French King,
however, had no desire to discuss the Prince's
future. So Charles wrote a memorandum in
which he pointed out that the penal measures
which the Hanoverian Government was taking
would ruin Scotland unless the King would
give him 20,000 regular troops with which to
go to the rescue. Lochiel was urging him to
press harder; but Louis merely offered him a
pension of 12,000 francs a month, which out-
raged his pride, and by November in a letter
to King James he was calling the French Ministers vermin. At the end of that month poor
old Sir Thomas Sheridan died, some said of
grief at the reproaches he had to bear from King
James. The King took advantage of the occasion to write to his elder son a long admonitory
letter on the subject of ill-advised friendships.

Charles has been much blamed for the
heartless way in which he declined to see his
father; but his awareness that everything done
and said at the Court in Rome was known

shortly afterwards by the Hanoverian Court and the Whig Government forced upon him a strict secrecy about his own plans. Moreover, Charles felt that his father's ambition to be King again had faded during all these weary years of hope deferred, and like all optimists he found the company of pessimists irritating.

Disgusted by the behaviour of the French, Charles went off to Spain, taking nobody into his confidence; but he was no more fortunate there than he had been in France. Charles now proposed to sue for the hand of the Czarina of Russia, who was a dozen years older than himself. One feels the despair behind such a fantastic notion and the passionate desire to redeem his promise that he would come back to Scotland. It was at this moment that James tried to reconcile him with Lord George Murray, and when the Prince declined to receive him his father rebuked him for 'conduct that was unchristian, unprincely, and impolitic.' All biographers have joined in condemning Charles for the lack of generosity he showed, but when one considers what a fatal influence Lord George Murray's had been upon the enterprise, and how little confidence Charles could have felt in the sincerity of his penitence, it is not difficult to excuse him.

If the Prince needed further evidence of human falsity his own brother was presently to supply it. On April 29th, 1747, Henry invited Charles to supper, having himself left Paris that afternoon. Charles waited until midnight in a state of great anxiety about Henry's disappearance, for he feared assassination. Three days later Charles received a letter to say that his brother had gone to Rome for a holiday. On June 13th James wrote to his son that His Holiness had offered a cardinal's hat to the Duke of York, and that the Duke of York had accepted it. This action was considered by all Jacobites a more mortal blow to the Cause than Culloden itself. The Principal of the Scots College in Paris wrote to the King's secretary in Rome that 'from the Prince to the lowest of his subjects all are unanimously crying out against what is done.'

Many years were to elapse before Charles would allow the Duke's health to be drunk, or even his name to be mentioned at his table.

It is at this date that for the first time we hear of the Prince in the role of a gallant. The chief lady in whom he was interested was the Princesse de Talmond, *née* Jablonowski, a Pole and a cousin of the Queen of France. She cannot have been less than forty and was probably more. Besides Madame de Talmond there were Madame de Montbazon, Madame de Guéménée, and the Duchess d'Aiguillon. The relations between Charles and these ladies has not yet been competently examined by any historian, and on the evidence at present available, there is nothing but scandal to suggest that the relationship between the Prince and them went beyond an intellectual intimacy. Indeed, the rage of despair into which Charles was thrown by his brother's plunge into perpetual celibacy suggests that Charles himself was not yet confident of his own ability to produce an heir, and the truth seems to be that his physical development was in one respect much retarded. To be sure, D'Argenson in his Memoirs definitely asserts that Madame de Talmond was the mistress of Charles. If that was the case, it would only add one to countless instances in which the woman of forty has influenced the development of a young man.

In the spring of 1748 the envoys of the various belligerent powers met at Aix-la-Chapelle to discuss terms of peace. One of the proposed clauses was to guarantee the succession of the crown of Great Britain to the House of Hanover, against which Charles protested formally to the French King in July, anticipating his own father in doing so, not a little to the annoyance of King James. When the preliminaries of the peace were signed Charles was officially notified of the probability of his having to quit French territory. His reply to this was to rent a large house opposite the Louvre and strike a medal with his own head on one side and on the other Britannia in the midst of a fleet circumscribed *Amor et Spes Britanniae*. This exasperated the French, who had just suffered a series of naval defeats at the hands of the British. It was a good instance of what Charles called his 'laconick manner of dealing with such vermin.'

Yet except with the Court and the Ministers Charles was the most popular figure in France. The knowledge that the House of Stuart was to be sacrificed as an added humiliation to France enraged public opinion, and Charles seems to have had some reason for writing to his father,

'I really do not think a peace so easy at present to be compassed as people are willing to flatter themselves with.' His popularity in Paris increased daily. He could not take a walk without being followed by an admiring crowd, and even his presence in the theatre diverted all attention from the play. Louis xv. began to grow nervous. He wrote to James in Rome that he had made arrangements for Charles to live in Switzerland, where he was to be provided with a pension and suitable guards. James ordered his son to fall in with the wishes of the French King. Charles paid no attention and treated the offer of a pension with contempt. Louis may have been beginning to feel a little anxiety about his own throne, and he determined to expel that inconveniently heroic figure from Paris.

Although Charles was privately informed that the warrant for his expulsion had been signed, he declined to leave Paris. The French authorities feared a popular rising. Twelve hundred of the guards under the Duc de Biron guarded the approaches to the Opera House. Troops lined the streets from the Palais Royal to Vincennes. Even scaling-ladders were provided for an attack on Charles's house. His military reputation is evident.

At a quarter-past five on the evening of December 11th Charles left his house accompanied by four gentlemen-in-waiting and drove to the Opera House. The moment the Prince alighted he was seized by several men and hurried along to a room on the ground floor of the Palais Royal, where he was disarmed and wound round with a quantity of silk ribbon which had been specially supplied. He was then carried to a coach, head foremost, and driven to the Château of Vincennes, where he was imprisoned for several days. It is related of him that he showed 'as much temper and magnanimity as any man could show in the height of prosperity, and even in his prison he appeared the monarch of the universe.' The French public were enraged when they heard of the treatment accorded to Charles. The Dauphin himself protested to his father, and it is not too much to say that when Louis signed the decree for Charles's expulsion he signed at the same time the death-warrant of the Bourbons.

On December 16th Charles, having been induced to promise the King in a letter that he would leave France, was set free, and he rode southward from Fontainebleau to Avignon, being well received in the Papal city, though he did upset the Archbishop by introducing boxing matches. England, however, was implacable. Avignon was held by the Hanoverian Government to be on French soil, and a demand was made at the Court of Versailles for Charles's expulsion. Versailles referred the matter to the Vatican, and when the Vatican declined to expel Charles the Anglo-Hanoverians threatened to bombard Città Vecchia, the port of Rome. This threat was communicated to Charles by the Vice-Legate, and on the night of February 28th, 1749, attended only by Colonel Henry Goring, he rode out of Avignon into that life of perpetual masquerade and obscure adventure, the details of which seem for ever lost.

The psychological development of Charles during his thirties is baffling. We hear of more ladies, such as Madame de Vassé and Mademoiselle Ferrand, and of a curious association of intellectuals who inhabited the residential part of a convent in the Rue Saint-Dominique, Paris. Here he seems to have divided his time between philosophic discussion with men like Condillac and Montesquieu and being the subject of quarrels among the various ladies.

For some time Charles had been very short of money; but suddenly we hear of his depositing 186,000 livres with Waters, his banker, and in June 1750 he is ordering an agent in Antwerp to buy him 26,000 muskets and other weapons. A month later he is writing to ask his father for a renewal of his commission as Regent. The Hanoverian Government was still much afraid of Charles. Only a few months earlier he had nearly been assassinated at Wurtzburg by a Whig agent. In May, Dr. King, the Principal of St. Mary's Hall at Oxford, who had not yet turned his coat for Hanoverian favours, made a speech at the opening of the Radcliffe which indicated the liveliest expectations of a glorious restoration. A new Jacobite medal was struck with a bust of Charles on one side and on the other a withered tree, of which one branch was sprouting into greenery with the legend *Revirescit*.

On September 12th Charles left Antwerp, arrived in London on the 16th, and without any warning walked into the drawing-room of

Lady Primrose in Essex Street, Strand, in the middle of a card party at which half the company were Whigs. After this he strolled round the Tower of London with a Colonel Brett, and discussed a project to seize it by a *coup de main*. He met fifty of his followers in a room in Pall Mall, including the Duke of Beaufort and the Earl of Westmorland, examined St. James's Palace, and wound up this extraordinary visit by being received into the Anglican Church either at St. Martin's-in-the-Fields or at St. Clement Dane's. Presumably he was not satisfied that the English Jacobites meant business, for on September 22nd he left London again.

The Prince's movements on his return to the Continent are shrouded for some time. Madame de Talmond, whom he now called the Queen of Morocco, was growing jealous of Mademoiselle Ferrand, and the end of that liaison was in sight. In February 1751 he paid a visit to Frederick the Great in Berlin. The Prussian King was polite, but would give no practical help, though he did appoint the Earl Marischal as his Ambassador to the Court of France.

That year, Alexander Murray, the younger brother of Lord Elibank, who had been charged with violence at the Westminster election, and afterwards put in gaol for refusing to beg the pardon of the House of Commons on his knees, left England, and in France declared himself a Jacobite. Not only this, but he proposed what came to be known as the Elibank Plot, which, like Christopher Layer's plot of thirty years earlier, was a project to kidnap the whole of the Hanoverian Royal Family. To this plot Lord Marischal was undoubtedly privy, though Charles was under no delusions about French or Prussian help. 'They mean to sell us as usual,' he wrote. However, Lord Marischal's presence at Versailles was always a menace to the usurper.

In spite of the quarrels over the Locharkaig treasure, by 1750 the bitterness roused by the Unclothing Act had made the Highlanders ready for another rising. This Act forbade 'any man or boy within that part of Great Britain called Scotland . . . on any pretext whatsoever, to wear or put on the clothes, commonly called Highland clothes, that is to say the plaid, filabeg or little kilt, trowse, shoul-

der belts, . . . and that no tartan or parti-col-
oured plaid or stuff should be used for greatcoats
or upper coats . . . every such person so
offending . . . shall suffer imprisonment for
six months, and being convicted of a second
offence shall be liable to be transported to any
of His Majesty's plantations beyond the seas,
there to remain for the space of seven years.'

In September 1750, Macdonnell of Lochgarry was writing to Sir Hector Maclean:

'. . . the Highlanders have had some smart en-
gagements with the regular troops, the former always getting the better. This all in defence of the
Highland clothes. God Almighty send these poor
people a respite, and an opportunity to show what
they would do to restore their King and relieve
their country. The troops have orders to kill upon
the spot any that's seen wear the least part of the
Highland garb. This cruelty makes all Highlanders of one thought . . .'

Lord George Murray, whom exile had made
more tolerant of forlorn hopes, was writing to
King James that the Highlanders would make
a powerful and useful diversion, especially if
they had a thousand men to support and
countenance their rising.

Cluny Macpherson was urging the Prince to

land again, and in 1751 the indomitable Alexander Macdonald published an edition of his poems, which was burnt by the common hangman in Edinburgh for their abuse of the usurping House.

By the early part of 1752 Charles was hard up again, and quarrelling with Madame de Talmond, who was becoming more and more jealous of Mademoiselle Ferrand. On top of this Madame de Vassé quarrelled with Charles, and he had to leave his comfortable nest in the convent. He was in these circumstances when he heard that Clementina Walkinshaw was residing in a Chapter of Canonesses in Flanders. It was she who had nursed him during his illness after the battle of Falkirk, and according to Elcho she had given herself to him at that time. What the fascination of Clementina was for Charles is an idle subject for speculation. It certainly existed, and to the disapproval of everybody he now sought her as a mistress. Clementina had a sister in the household of Frederick, the *de facto* Prince of Wales. This aroused Jacobite suspicion, and by a sinister coincidence very shortly after Miss Walkinshaw joined the Prince it became evident to

Jacobites that their most intimate plans were being betrayed to the Hanoverian Government.

There is no space to set forth at length the evidence which fixes the guilt on Macdonell of Glengarry and demonstrates his identity with Pickle the Spy. The case which Andrew Lang made out against him cannot be refuted. Not only did Alasdair Ruadh, as he was called, betray every detail of the Elibank Plot, but he was the most notable double-dealer in the matter of the Locharkaig gold. The day fixed for the kidnapping of the Hanoverian Royal Family was November 10th, 1752. Glengarry was to command four hundred Highlanders for this occasion. The enterprise was postponed. Lochgarry and Dr. Archibald Cameron went over to Scotland to get more of that miserable Locharkaig gold for the Prince, and, betrayed by Pickle, Dr. Cameron was arrested in March 1753. He was not tried for participation in the Elibank Plot, which was never mentioned, but for his share in the '45. The Government was anxious not to let the Jacobites know what a valuable confidant it possessed in Pickle. Dr. Cameron was condemned to death, and on

June 7th, 1753, he was hanged at Tyburn, but by a gracious act of His Hanoverian Majesty not disembowelled. 'Never did man make a more glorious exit. He met the last great enemy with as much intrepidity and as much decency as even the great Balmerino.' The judicial murder of Dr. Cameron was execrated by the Whigs themselves, and it is clear the Government must have been seriously frightened by the favourable prospect at that moment of a Stuart Restoration to risk so much unpopularity. With the martyrdom of Dr. Cameron and the treachery of Pickle the Elibank Plot fizzled out.

The shock to Charles's hopes was violent. The next two years were among the most wretched in his life. The influence of Clementina Walkinshaw seems to have been entirely evil, and the death of Mademoiselle Ferrand removed the last link with his earlier and more attractive feminine society. It seems probable, moreover, that about now his brain began to be affected by the nervous strain of the last ten years. Charles took refuge from misfortune in drink, and, although no woman might have been able to console him for the life of action of which he was thwarted, another than Clementina Walkinshaw might have known how not to make bad worse. The first serious quarrel with her seems to have been over the baptism of their daughter Charlotte, who was born on October 29th, 1753. Clementina naturally desired that she should be baptized as a Catholic; but Charles, still clinging to his 'conversion' to Anglicanism, wanted his daughter to be a Protestant. In his rage he actually contemplated the dismissal of his Catholic Highland servants, and was ready to discard his mistress because she was a Papist. The letter he wrote to Goring acquainting him of this resolution is that of a man temporarily bereft of sanity. Yet only a year later he was writing to his father's secretary when in straits for money and recommending his servants to the King's good offices. Of one Duncan, a footman, he wrote, 'The latter, tho' noways fitting for service, deserves particular attention; he was a poor shepherd in Cameron's Clan that was of service to me when I was skulking in the Highlands.'

Presently, Charles's health improved, and the reconciliation with his mistress may have been helped by the attempts of his friends to separate him from Clementina, who was by now established in Jacobite opinions as a dangerous spy. The Hanoverian Government, knowing that Charles was in a wretched way, hounded him from place to place on the Continent with spies and assassins, and at one moment we hear of him disguised as a Capuchin friar to escape his enemies. The life he was leading, harassed for want of money, disappointed in all his projects, and out of sympathy with the woman with whom he had involved himself, brought out in him all that was capricious and perverse. His friends were alienated. The devoted Henry Goring resigned from his service in May 1754, on which Charles wrote to complain about him to the Earl Marischal. Lord Marischal, who had never liked Charles personally, and who had always refused his help when it was asked, wrote a stern letter of rebuke for his behaviour to Goring. One sentence from the reply of the unhappy Prince might have moved even Whig biographers to charity:

'My heart is broke enough without that you should finish it, your expressions are so strong without knowing where.'

During these months of lonely despair the Prince at last abandoned the hope of that return to Scotland for which so many faithful hearts had been waiting. On September 4th, 1754, he wrote to Cluny Macpherson:

'For C. M. in Scotld.

'SIR,—This is to desire to come as soon as you can conveniently to Paris, bringing over with you all the effects whatsoever that I left in your hands when I was in Scotland, and also whatever money you can come at, for I happen to be at present in great straits. . . . You are to address yourself when arrived at Paris to Mr. John Waters, Banker, &c. He will direct you where to find your sincere friend,   C. P.'

About a year later Cluny made an attempt to persuade the Prince to give up the society of his mistress, and put before him in a long memoir the various scandals which were alienating the support of his friends. Unfortunately, this memoir was based on slanders circulated by James Dawkins, who had been employed by Charles as an envoy in Berlin, and who, like so many friends, had turned against him. The Prince's pride would not allow him to defend himself. He replied coldly.

In 1755-56 Charles was living at Basle under

the name of Dr. Thomson. The outbreak of
the Seven Years' War awakened Jacobite hopes
again. Lord George Murray wrote optimistic-
ally to King James's secretary. There was some
question of offering Charles the leadership of
the attack on Minorca in April 1757; but he
declined it. 'The English will do me justice
if they think fit,' he said, 'but I will no longer
serve as a mere bugbear.' Few men indeed had
acquired by bitter experience such a nice judgment of the political methods of France. In
1759 there was a project to invade England.
At Rouen flat-bottomed boats were built for
the troops, under Marshal de Belle Isle, and
Charles drew up a proclamation asseverating
his renunciation of the Catholic Chuch. However, Hawke's victory in Quiberon Bay put an
end to further schemes of an invasion.

In July 1760, Clementina Walkinshaw left
Charles and took refuge in the Convent of
Meaux, taking her daughter with her. They
had grown to hate one another, and though it
would be over-credulous to believe all the
squalid details which the enemies of Charles
took delight in circulating, there is no doubt
that the association was without beauty. That

autumn the Third George was crowned King.

We hear little of Charles's movements during the next five years. There is one pathetic letter in which he alludes to his 'Scotch blood' and 'shivers to think of a report that the Scotch regiments are to be reformed.' Many Highlanders wore the red coat now. It was the only coat with which they could wear their own dress. Some of those who had fought at Culloden had fought at Quebec.

In 1765 the Cardinal Duke of York, foreseeing that the old King would not live much longer, attempted a reconciliation with his brother. Charles replied through a secretary that he was willing to be reconciled with Henry, but that he did not wish to see any one. His Royal Eminence tried again, and informed his brother that he proposed to renounce all the bequests to him under their father's will in favour of Charles. He went on to mention the Princess de Talmond, who was then in Rome. 'She always speaks of Your Royal Highness with the greatest regard and respect, and really seems to be sincerely attached to you. She complains she never can hear of you, and thinks she deserves a share in your remembrance.'

Finally, Charles made up his mind to go back to Rome and receive his father's blessing before he died. He left Paris on December 30th, 1765, to make that return journey to the city which he had left with such high hopes nearly twenty-two years before. He arrived too late to see his father alive.

James III. died on the night of January 1st, 1766, after a reign *in partibus* of sixty-four years, the longest of any British monarch. He was a good man, and in the beauty and piety of his personal life he deserves to be coupled with Henry VI., whose claims for canonization have for long been pleaded. That he was never *de facto* King of Scotland, England, France, and Ireland must be regarded as an irreparable loss, for which the full penalty has perhaps not even yet been paid by the countries that rejected him:

'Farewell, O Pious Prince! the palm is won.
The everlasting crown of bliss thy own.
Why should I weep thy fate? Alas! thy life
Was one continued scene of injury and grief.
Thou, blameless infant, from her aether driv'n,
Long mourned her woes. Now freed from wo'
  you rise,
But poor Britannia in dishonour lies!'

137

XII

CHARLES III

THE first business of the Cardinal was to attempt to obtain the recognition of his brother as King Charles III. from the Holy See; but the British Government, in spite of the home-bred produce it now owned as King, still feared Charles, and the Vatican was not prepared to face English hostility. The Royal Arms above the Palazzo Muti were ordered to be taken down. The Cardinal was severely reprimanded by the Pope for driving into Rome with his brother seated on his right, a mark of respect which cardinals should only give to reigning sovereigns. Other dignitaries who paid him royal honours were reprimanded, and the Rectors of the Scots, English, and Irish Colleges in Rome were banished for acknowledging him as King. The usual lying gossip was written home about Charles's behaviour by Horace Mann, the egregious British envoy to the petty court of the Grand Duke of Tuscany, but there is a letter in existence from Sir William Hamilton, the British envoy at Naples, which contradicts malicious report. 'The life he leads is now very regular and sober. His chief occupation is shooting in the environs of Rome.' Hamilton goes on to quote the description given him by an English lady who had just seen Charles in Rome. 'As for his person it is rather handsome, his face ruddy and full of pimples. He looks good-natured and was overjoyed to see me—nothing could be more affectionately gracious. I cannot answer for his cleverness, for he appeared to me to be absorbed in melancholy thoughts, a good deal of distraction in his conversation and frequent brown studies . . . he has all the reason in the world to be melancholy, for there is not a soul goes near him, not knowing what to call him. He told me time lay heavy upon him . . . he depends entirely for his substance upon his brother.'

It was at his time of loneliness that Charles was reconciled with the Princess de Talmond. 'Mon tendre amitié pour vous, Madame,' he wrote, 'était toujours gravé en mon cœur.' She was old now, and pious. Horace Walpole had visited her in the Luxembourg and found her in a gloomy room surrounded by cats and pictures of saints and Sobieskis.

After a while this self-imposed solitude began to weary Charles, and he decided to enter Roman society, taking the title Count Albany. He even allowed his brother to arrange an audience with the Pope as a private nobleman. Presumably about now he abandoned his attempts to persuade people that he was a member of the Anglican Church. Music was his main diversion, as indeed it had been all his life, and about this time he took up the study of the French horn. There were occasional relapses into drinking bouts, which of course were exaggerated by enemies. The 'grog-blossoms' which the English lady noted were evidently transient, for in 1769 we hear 'that not a blot nor so much as a pimple was in his face, though maliciously given out by some that it was all over blotted; but he is jolly and plump, though not to excess, being still agile and fit for undergoing toil.' In this year Mrs. Forbes, the wife of Bishop Forbes, the devoted compiler of *The Lyon in Mourning*, sent a piece of seed-cake to Charles by two Jacobite travellers. 'Ay!' said he, 'a piece of cake from Scotland and from Edinburgh too!' Then rising from his seat and opening a drawer, 'Here,' said he, 'you see me deposit it, and no teeth shall go upon it but my own.'

Meanwhile, over in England the Third George had declared himself a true-born Briton, to the disgust of all true-born Englishmen. No doubt the emphasis on being a Briton was due to his chief Minister, the wily Lord Bute, the lover of George's mother and himself a left-handed Stuart. A good time was coming for Scotsmen, and the benefits of the Union were beginning to be appreciated when the humblest Scot could aspire to be Archbishop of Canterbury. Yet Jacobitism was not dead. So late as 1777 that great and good man Dr. Johnson observed: 'If England were fairly polled, the present King would be sent away to-night, and his adherents hanged to-morrow.'

The French, worried by reverses, began to think it would be as well to have a youthful 'Pretender' as a rod in pickle for the English. With this end in view French intrigue tempted Charles into marriage by promising subsidies and suggesting the probability of Papal recognition. The choice was Princess Louise of Stolberg, a girl of eighteen, who occupied a Canoness's stall in the exclusive Chapter of Mons. She was connected with many of the leading houses of European nobility, and on her mother's side was descended from Robert Bruce. Louise was a young lady of ambition, and the effort which writers like Vernon Lee have made to sentimentalize her character completely failed. She was indeed a hussy.

The wedding took place at Macerata on Good Friday, 1772. By a significant clause in the marriage contract Charles was obliged to consummate the marriage that same night. This was insisted upon by Louise's mother, and almost the first thing we hear of the innocent young bride is her recommending the use of rouge to the ladies of Charles's household.

On April 22nd, Charles and Louise entered Rome. The Cardinal Duke of York did his best to give the entry a regal appearance with outriders in scarlet liveries and white cockades, and to the bride he presented a snuff-box set in diamonds inside which was a draft for 40,000 crowns. Although no recognition was given by the Papal Court, Roman society welcomed them, and Louise was allowed the Royal privilege of not returning calls.

Clementina Walkinshaw, who now called herself the Countess Alberstrof, took advantage of the embarrassment her presence might cause in Rome at this date by arriving there with her daughter Charlotte, who was a few months older than the *de jure* Queen. The Cardinal granted them a small pension, and presently they returned to the convent at Meaux.

There is no doubt that Charles was now making a great effort to lead a life of which not even his enemies could make capital, and perhaps if Louise had been able to produce an heir all would have gone well. There were no signs of that happy event, however, and by the end of 1773 Charles was reported to be drinking again. The following year he and Louise moved to Florence, much to the irritation of the Grand Duke of Tuscany, who had not even the courtesy to acknowledge Charles as Count Albany. Here, too, Louise's airs and graces seem to have offended the ladies of the Florentine nobility, who finding she would not call on them ceased to call on her. The result was that her salon was always full of men, which made her husband jealous. He was still hoping for a son, and his House having suffered from two aspersions on its births, he was fearful of the slightest reflection on Louise's honour. To this was added the nervous irritation of feeling that spies were covertly watching the figure and the complexion of his wife in order to post off the news of her pregnancy and prepare a putative father for the child.

In this atmosphere the relations of Charles and Louise grew strained. Their tastes differed. He loved music. She cared not at all for music, but much for pictures. The defenders of the 'Queen of Hearts' have made much play with the sad situation of a girl exposed to the embraces of a drunkard much older than herself. Yet Louise herself gives the lie to such sentimentality. In June 1775 she is writing to reproach Charles for making her go for walks with him in the heat, and taunts him for wanting her to get up at seven o'clock in the morning after not going to bed till two. 'It would not redound to your honour in the world, sir,' she writes, 'if it were known that you who have always passed as so stout a fellow (gaillard) should have become so degenerate as not to want to spend more than a few hours in bed with a pretty young woman who loves you.' She goes on in this letter to sneer at the 'Face Royal,' and she even threatens Charles with publishing to the world all the intimate facts of their married life together.

The effect on Charles of such a wife was naturally to make him drink more heavily, and to the effects of alcohol were added asthma and warnings of apoplexy.

Yet, even still his name meant something, and there is evidence that once or twice during the war between England and the American Colonies there were suggestions of offering him a crown in Boston, while at a strike of coal-heavers in Newcastle he was proclaimed King as Charles III.

In 1777 the carroty-haired poet Vittorio Alfieri appeared on the scene, and in order to justify himself for the seduction of Louise spat calumny. The climax was reached on St. Andrew's Day, 1780, when Charles, who had been celebrating the patron saint of Scotland, broke into his wife's bedroom, and according to her tried to strangle her; but this assertion may have been an excuse for leaving Charles. Her escape was managed by Alfieri himself with a stage Irishman and his elderly Italian mistress.

Louise found asylum in a convent, and put herself under the protection of the Grand Duchess of Tuscany. From here she wrote to the Cardinal Duke, who, simple man, believed her story and advised her to retire to a convent in Rome, the very convent to which Queen Clementina had retired after making false accusations against King James.

For a time Louise carried off the situation, and Alfieri to avoid scandal kept out of Rome. The Cardinal was so much moved by the distresses of his sister-in-law that he reduced Charles's pension by half and gave the money to her instead. She also managed to get an allowance of 20,000 crowns a year from France. Alfieri, who had had the courage to challenge an elderly invalid to a duel, now arrived in Rome, where the eloquence inspired by his platonic affection charmed even the Pope. Charles, who through his wife's behaviour had been reduced to poverty, comported himself in such a dignified way that not even the interminable Mann could find anything in his behaviour to criticize. He sent a dignified protest to the Vatican in December 1782, asking for his full pension and the banishment of Count Alfieri from Rome.

Early in 1783 Charles became ill, so seriously ill that he was given the last Sacraments and made his will. He appointed as his heiress his daughter, Charlotte Stuart. On March 30th he secured her legitimation, and gave her the title of Duchess of Albany. On hearing of his brother's illness the Cardinal set out to Florence, where Charles satisfied him that the friendship between Alfieri and his wife was a guilty liaison. The Cardinal communicated with the Pope, and Alfieri was ordered to leave Rome within a fortnight.

Charles recovered from his illness and continued to eke out in Florence a solitary life. His only consolation now was music. He used to sit for hours in a large gloomy room hung with crimson damask and lighted by two candles, playing to himself old tunes on the violoncello or the bagpipe or the French horn. On the table there were always two loaded pistols. Sometimes a music-master would acccompany him on the harpsichord, and the music would come to an end by the playing of 'Lochaber No More,' at which he always broke down and wept. The disease of the brain took its relentless course. He was oppressed by the fear of beggary, haunted by visions from the past of the martyrs of Carlisle and York and Kennington and the bloody heather of Culloden Moor.

In the autumn of this melancholy year the amiable and well-disposed Gustavus III. of Sweden visited Charles in Florence, and after going into his finances arranged in Rome a formal separation between Charles and Louise. By the terms of this Louise gave up her 'pin-money,' which by her marriage contract was 15,000 livres a year, and also the 4000 crowns that was her share of the Pope's pension. She had for some time been writing letters to Alfieri, despairing of her husband's death. Soon after the separation she went to live openly with her lover, with whom she remained until 1803, and when he died she immediately took as her acknowledged lover the young French painter, Fabre.

It was now that Charles turned to his daughter Charlotte. In July 1784 she joined him in Florence, and over the last three or four years of his life she shed a few late golden rays of affection and understanding. When Clementina Walkinshaw had left him just twenty-four years ago, Charles had made several efforts to secure for himself the care of his child; but, owing to the fear that he intended to bring her up as a Protestant, King James himself had intervened and insisted that Clementina should keep her daughter. Charlotte had corresponded in French with her father, and Charles, true to his lifelong principle of 'all or nothing,' had treated with some harshness those long ill-spelt appeals for money.

Charlotte was a tall handsome young woman of over thirty now, with a good deal of the tomboy about her. She was utterly without affectation, but had much tact and a sweet disposition. Her poor old father was delighted with her. He gave dinner parties in her honour, bought her expensive gowns, and went riding with her every day. Charlotte, who had spent a dull life in the convent at Meaux, was as happy as a schoolgirl on a holiday. Gradually she succeeded in keeping her father away from the bottle. She made friends with her uncle, the Cardinal, first in letters and then at a personal meeting. Charles celebrated St. Andrew's Day, 1774, by a large dinner party in Charlotte's honour and the formal investiture of her with the green ribbon of the Order. Away over in Scotland Robert Burns heard the news, and wrote:

'My heart is wae, and unco wae,
To think upon the raging sea
That roars between her gardens green
And the bonie Lass of Albany.
This lovely maid's of royal blood
That ruled Albion's kingdoms three,
But oh, alas, for her bonie face,
They've wranged the Lass of Albany.'

None knew better than the Bonny Lass of Albany herself what Scotland meant to her father. One day an Englishman called Greathead visited Charles and drew him on into telling over again the old story of the '45. All went well until he came to Culloden. Then with the memory of the slaughter, the hangings, the floggings, the exiles, and of all that his enterprise had cost his country, he fell from his chair in a fit upon the floor. His daughter, hearing the noise, came in. 'O Sir,' she cried, 'what is this? You must have been speaking to my father about Scotland and the Highlands.

No one dares to mention these subjects in his presence.'

Charles was ageing very rapidly. At the end of 1785 it was suggested by the Cardinal that he and the Duchess should come and live in Rome. Charles, who in the old days had only to receive such a suggestion to make him oppose it, was delighted to do as his daughter wanted. The Pope acknowledged her rank and her legitimation, which was a pleasure and pride to her father, and compensated for the discourtesy shown to Charlotte by the wretched little Grand Duke of Tuscany and his Duchess.

In the spring of 1786 Charles was affected with a dropsy; but by the summer he was well enough to go to Albano, where he touched many poor people for the King's Evil. In Rome that winter he suffered from a severe shock. The Comte de Vaudreuil, son of the officer who had arrested Charles at the Opera House in Paris that December evening nearly forty years ago, waited upon him to pay his respects. The name meant nothing to Charles; but when the Count, who much resembled his father, came in, his appearance reconjured in

Charles's mind that dreadful night of humiliation, and he dropped to the floor in a fit.

For two years in that old Palazzo where he had been born Charles lingered on. Music was still his consolation, and as he sat nodding and listening to the old Gaelic tunes he loved, we may hope that through his decaying brain flashed happy visions of the past, of that white beach on Eriskay, of the blue mountains beyond Arisaig and Moidart, of the silken Standard beside Loch Shiel, and that faint as the whisper in a dusty shell he heard again the great war pipes skirling and the cheering crowds in Edinburgh and the sound of oars on Hebridean seas and the babble of brown moorland burns and the wind in the heather. It is little enough to hope for one who himself hoped so dauntlessly.

At the beginning of January 1788 a paralytic stroke deprived the King of the use of one-half of his body, and between nine and ten o'clock on the anniversary of King Charles the Martyr he died [1] in the arms of his daughter. The Cardinal Duke of York, now by the grace of God, but not by the desire of men, King Henry I. of Scotland and IX. of England, France, and

[1] The death was kept secret until January 31st.

Ireland, asked the Pope to grant a Royal funeral in St. Peter's. It was refused. In his own diocese of Frascati the Cardinal performed the obsequies.

Charlotte did not survive her father long. In 1789 she died from a malady brought on by a fall from her horse. In that year fell the Bastille, and fortune's malice turned against the faithless House of Bourbon.

EPILOGUE

IN the remote Highland parish of Gairloch, William Ross, a young Skye poet, wrote the Prince's only elegy, and this was what Charles himself would have wished.

An Suaithneas Bàn (*The White Cockade*) is free from the unreal sentiment of the Lowland songs that were so eloquent when the Cause was lost. The youth of the Highlands, they who had never seen the Prince, still hoped that his war-cry would be heard again, and his fleet be seen upon the ocean sailing to redeem his people. With his death that hope was finally extinguished. And then, after imploring God not to exact vengeance for the wrong done to the White Cockade, with the vision granted to a poet William Ross sees that, despite the promises of Divine favours in the mouths of good ministers, the loss of the White Cockade must bring ruin upon Scotland.

The young poet did not live to see his

prophecy fulfilled to the uttermost. Two years later he himself followed the White Cockade to Tir nan Òg.

BIBLIOGRAPHY

It has not been thought desirable to overload a brief biography like this with footnotes giving chapter and verse for every statement, but a list of the principal authorities consulted may be of interest.

Historical Papers relating to the Jacobite Period, edited by Colonel James Allardyce. 2 vols.

The Albemarle Papers, edited by Charles Sanford Terry. 2 vols.
Useful for details of military and civil administration of Scotland immediately after Culloden.

Itinerary of Prince Charles Edward Stuart, by Walter Biggar Blaikie.
An indispensable diary with some valuable supplementary matter and a splendid map illustrating the Prince's movements.

Origins of the 'Forty-Five and other Papers relating to that Rising, edited by Walter Biggar Blaikie.
Another indispensable work which includes the narrative of Captain Daniel who joined the Prince in Lancashire.

Culloden Papers. The correspondence of Duncan Forbes. Five supplementary volumes have been published recently.

Affairs of Scotland by David, Lord Elcho, 1744-46. With a Memoir and Annotations by the Hon. Evan Charteris.
A model of accurate editing.

BIBLIOGRAPHY

The History of the Rebellion in the Year 1745, by
  John Home.

The author of *Douglas* was one of the Edinburgh
volunteers. Written with a Whig bias, but the appendix contains some important documents.

Memoirs of the Rebellion in 1745-46, by the Chevalier
  de Johnstone.

This puts the case for Lord George Murray, and
is a lively if unreliable piece of work.

The Lyon in Mourning, by the Rev. Robert Forbes,
  A.M., Bishop of Ross and Caithness. Edited by
  Henry Paton. 3 vols.

The compiler was arrested on his way to join the
Prince in September 1745 and not released until 1746.
He therefore had an opportunity in prison of obtain-
ing the narratives of many of the principal characters
in the Rising, and when he was released he devoted
the rest of his life to collecting material. He was a
man of the strictest probity, and every item of infor-
mation was severely tested by him before he included
it in his monumental collection. This work is the
foundation-stone of our knowledge of the 'Forty-Five.

The Lockhart Papers. 2 vols.

The second volume includes the anonymous journal
and memoir by a Highland writer who the present
writer is satisfied was Alexander Macdonald, the
Gaelic poet.

Memorials of John Murray of Broughton, edited by
  Robert Fitzroy Bell.

Another indispensable work admirably edited.

*Narrative of Charles, Prince of Wales' Expedition to
  Scotland in the Year* 1745, by James Maxwell of
  Kirkconnell.

Savagely biassed against Murray of Broughton.

BIBLIOGRAPHY

A Compleat History of the Rebellion, by James Ray.
A coarse and scurrilous work by a ruffian who committed several acts of brutality after Culloden. It contains a racy description of Edinburgh.

The Woodhouselee MS., edited by A. Francis Steuart. Prejudiced but extremely racy.

A Royalist Family, Irish and French (1689-1789), *and Prince Charles Edward,* translated by A. G. Murray Macgregor.
Contains the Prince's correspondence with Anthony Walsh, and the log of the *Du Teillay.*

Browne's History of the Highlands and of the Highland Clans, including an Appendix of *Stuart Papers.* 4 vols.
A most useful work.

Lord Macleod's Narrative, in Sir William Fraser's *Earls of Cromartie.*

List of Persons Concerned in the Rebellion, edited by Lord Rosebery and the Rev. Walter Macleod.

History of the Rebellion, 1745-46, by Robert Chambers.
Sympathetic and accurate.

Lord George Murray and the 'Forty-Five, by Winifred Duke.
A careful edition of Lord George's correspondence, but the narrative portion is without historical or literary value, and the tone is that of an angry governess.

Life and Times of Prince Charles Edward, by Charles Alexander Ewald.
A painstaking compilation, but often inaccurate, and written with a flow of snivelling morality which becomes nauseous.

Essays on the Superstitions of the Highlands of Scotland, by Mrs. Grant of Laggan.
Worth consulting for the insight into the Highlander's point of view.

James Francis Edward, The Old Chevalier, by Martin Haile.
A solid and dignified piece of work.

Memoirs of the Jacobites and Their Adherents, by John Heneage Jesse. 3 vols.

Prince Charles Edward, by Andrew Lang.
Particularly valuable for the early and later years of the Prince. Often careless over dates and names, and written in a donnish style.

Pickle the Spy, or the Incognito of Prince Charles, by Andrew Lang.

The Companions of Pickle, by Andrew Lang.
Both these volumes make lamentable reading for the enthusiast, but are indispensable.

The Countess of Albany, by Vernon Lee.
The case for the hussy.

History of England from the Peace of Utrecht to the Peace of Aix-la-Chapelle, by Lord Mahon. 3 vols.

The Decline of the Last Stuarts; Extracts from the Despatches of British Envoys to the Secretary of State, edited for the Roxburghe Club by Lord Mahon.

Journal and Memoirs of the Marquis D'Argenson, by E. J. B. Rathery. 2 vols.
Essential for the later life of Charles.

History of England, comprising the Reign of Queen Anne until the Peace of Utrecht, by Earl Stanhope.

BIBLIOGRAPHY

Tales of a Century; or, Sketches of the Romance of History between the years 1746 *and* 1846, by John Sobieski and Charles Edward Stuart.
Contains much interesting, but not always trustworthy material.

A Court in Exile, by Marchesa Vitelleschi. 2 vols.
Sentimental and tiresome, but contains useful material.

Life and Adventures of Prince Charles Edward Stuart, by W. D. Norie. 4 vols.
This is by far the best life of the Prince for popular reading. It contains invaluable photographs of places and relics, and it is the only modern life written with true compassion. It is useless, however, for the later years of the Prince.

A Series of Letters, by Oliver MacAllester.
This production by a spy may be consulted with discretion for details of the projected invasion of 1759.

William Augustus, Duke of Cumberland, by the Hon. Evan Charteris.
This puts the case for the Butcher as favourably as possible, and gives a good picture of the times.

The Loyal Clans, by Audrey Cunningham.
A scholarly and conscientious piece of work.

The Jacobite Movement, by Sir Charles Petrie.
Contains the best account of the Elibank Plot.

INDEX

INDEX

166

INDEX

(1)